YOUR DAILY VEG

YOUR DAILY VEG

Joe Woodhouse
Modern, fuss-free vegetarian food

Kyle Books

An Hachette UK Company
www.hachette.co.uk

First published in Great Britain in 2022 by
Kyle Books, an imprint of Octopus Publishing Group Limited
Carmelite House
50 Victoria Embankment
London EC4Y 0DZ
www.kylebooks.co.uk
www.octopusbooksusa.com

ISBN: 978 0 85783 9664

Text copyright © Joe Woodhouse 2022
Design and layout copyright
© Octopus Publishing Group Limited 2022
Photography copyright © Joe Woodhouse 2022

Distributed in the US by Hachette Book Group,
1290 Avenue of the Americas,
4th and 5th Floors, New York, NY 10104

Distributed in Canada by Canadian Manda Group,
664 Annette St., Toronto, Ontario, Canada M6S 2C8

Publishing Director **Judith Hannam**
Publisher **Joanna Copestick**
Copy Editor **Claire Rogers**
Editorial Assistant **Zakkaria Raja**
Designer **Helen Bratby**
Photographer **Joe Woodhouse**
Production **Emily Noto**

A Cataloguing in Publication record for this
title is available from the British Library

Printed and bound in China

10 9 8 7 6 5 4 3 2 1

Acknowledgements

For my father

Thank you to my parents for giving me freedom
to pursue my passions. However worrying that
may have sometimes been.

My wonderful wife, Olia, for her relentless
enthusiasm, encouragement and appetite.

Thank you Emily Sweet for ever being such
a source of grounding guidance and believing
in me.

To everyone at Kyle Books for working so hard
on the book. For helping me get down on paper
and show what I wanted to. For the freedom
and encouragement. Thank you. It was such
a pleasure to work with you all and it was
glorious to see everything come together.

Helen Bratby for such a wonderful design.
It really made this book for me. Thank you.

Thank you Anna, Nigella & Rachel for such
flattering words. They fill me with pride.

To all the people who have cooked for or
with me and passed on skills or knowledge
unwittingly or not.

To anyone that is in the position to share their
experience and knowledge that spend that little
extra time to help someone fully understand.

CONTENTS

Introduction

Vegetarian and vegan food has often been labelled boring, stodgy and bland. I want to create dishes that are visually appealing but, crucially, even better to eat. **Recipes that really satisfy, built from good quality ingredients that are allowed to speak for themselves** and, most importantly, can be enjoyed by everyone, regardless of whether you eat meat or not. **Nothing faddy, just decent, wholehearted food that is cooked well, with an exciting layering of textures, spices and flavours**, and which, as is often said by my Ukrainian, meat-loving father-in-law, mean you don't even think about the lack of meat.

I became a vegetarian at the age of ten. It wasn't a dietary thing or a fad – growing up on a farm, that would have been dismissed pretty quickly – but rather the result of a sudden awareness of the food I was consuming and what felt right to me. My parents embraced my decision and indulged their son's newfound quirk, my mother attempting, on occasion, to marry elements of my new dietary requirements with our evening meals. I felt, though, that I shouldn't impose my choices on them – nor the extra burden of cooking another separate meal on my mother – so I set about teaching myself to cook. Easing in on a basic level, I either asked advice or taught myself using books and tips picked up from cookery shows, gradually progressing to more advanced techniques. There were a fair few disasters, but mostly as a result of trying too hard and adding too many components. Over the years I have strived to refine and pare down this initial eagerness to arrive at the way I cook today.

Most of the time I work backwards from an ingredient, as opposed to starting with a specific dish or recipe. If something looks especially good it may nudge out other ingredients, or indeed whole dishes, to allow what is at its best to take centre stage. I like to showcase a vegetable as a main ingredient, supporting its flavour with complementary combinations, and a lot of my cooking involves of-the-moment concoctions that take shape from what is at hand.

I'm happiest when there are a decent number of people around to feed – largely because it allows for many big platters that get passed around and eaten with gusto, but also because cooking for a crowd is rewarding and lots of fun. The whole gamut of cultures and traditions fascinate me, and coming together around the table to share food is at the heart of this. **No matter where I go in the world, the recurring ethos seems to be: the best quality ingredients, tampered with as little as possible, and presented in simple ways.** My cooking reflects this: straightforward food that is more than the sum of its parts.

I went on to train as a chef and spent a number of years working in kitchens, as well at events and festivals. More recently, my work as a food and travel photographer has allowed me to gather a huge amount of knowledge, of tastes and cooking methods, both at home and much farther afield. I have endeavoured to pass on as many tips as possible, be it advice on cooking techniques or recommendations on how best to prep dishes in order to minimise stress and time in the kitchen when guests are present. **Because of the nature of my recipes – which are a celebration of seasonal ingredients at their peak – they lend themselves to being eaten as multi-course meals or grouped together as offerings for larger groups for feasting or barbecues. Often dishes can as easily be eaten off platters as individually plated. Do add simple boiled grains, or rice to help build them into full meals.** What I have aimed to create with this book is something that is properly useful for the people cooking from it, a book that will be used and loved.

POTATOES CARROTS & BEETROOT

A wonderful platform for other flavours but a worthy star of the show in their own right, **POTATOES** cooked in any way are brilliant. Whenever we head off to go camping or to stay in a cottage, I'm sure to take some small and large potatoes. They are so easy to build a meal around: simply steam or boil. Like most vegetables, if they are grown well, all they need is some butter or oil and few handfuls of fresh herbs.

Potato farls

When I used to get the ferry to Ireland as a child, one of the highlights for me was the farls in the breakfast on the early morning crossing. They're such a wonderful addition to a hearty breakfast and a great base for a lunch plate with a fried egg.

SERVES 4 AS PART OF A BREAKFAST OR LUNCH

- 500g (1lb 2oz) cooked potatoes, coarsely mashed or leftover mashed potato
- 100g (3½oz) unsalted butter, melted
- 100g (3½oz) plain flour
- ½ teaspoon bicarbonate of soda
- 2 spring onions, finely sliced (optional)
- sea salt flakes and black pepper

1. Mix together the potatoes, butter, flour, bicarbonate of soda and spring onions, if using, in a bowl with salt and pepper to taste. Everything should be well combined.

2. On a lightly floured work surface, flatten out the mixture to a roughly 34 × 22cm (13½ × 8½ inch) rectangle. Cut into 8 even pieces.

3. Heat a heavy-based frying pan or cast-iron griddle pan over a medium/medium-low heat. Place the farls in the pan and gently cook them for 4–6 minutes until golden. Flip and cook the second side in a similar fashion. They are done when they are cooked through and fluffy inside.

Sweet potato & ginger stew with quinoa

I was introduced to this dish by my friend, wonderful chef Paola Carosella. It has such a freshness and vibrancy to it. Paola originally made this as a soup, but I lean towards a more stew-like consistency. If you prefer a soupier version, add more water accordingly. The longer this sits, the deeper the flavours will develop – so happily make it ahead of time.

SERVES 6

- 2 onions, sliced Lyonnaise (see intro on page 137)
- 3 tablespoons oil
- 6 garlic cloves, peeled
- 50g (1¾oz) fresh root ginger, peeled
- 2 star anise
- 1 cinnamon stick
- 8 tomatoes, roughly diced, or 2 × 400g (14oz) cans chopped tomatoes
- 4 sweet potatoes (about 600g/1lb 5oz), cut into 2.5cm (1 inch) chunks
- 150g (5½oz) quinoa, any colour
- sea salt flakes

TO SERVE
- mozzarella or stringy cheese (optional)
- yoghurt (if not using cheese)
- red chilli, sliced
- fresh coriander, leaves picked
- 6 limes, cut into quarters

1. Sauté the onions with the oil and a decent couple of pinches of salt in a heavy-based saucepan over medium heat for 15 minutes until translucent. Add a splash of water if they go too dry.

2. Crush the garlic under the heel of your knife and throw it into the pan as is. Grate the ginger directly into the pan using a fine or medium grater (or finely chop and add to the pan). Add the spices. Sauté for a further 2 minutes until the onions have fully softened.

3. Add the tomatoes along with water from half-filling the cans and rinsing them out, then cook for 10 minutes.

4. Add the sweet potato chunks and gently simmer for 20–30 minutes or until they are tender when poked with a knife. Keep topping up the water if needed. Check the seasoning when they are done.

5. Cook the quinoa in salted boiling water for 15 minutes. Usually I cook and drain quinoa ahead of time, refreshing it in cold water to stop the cooking process. When the stew is ready, stir in the cooked quinoa to warm through. Add a touch of water, if necessary.

6. In suitable bowls, add the diced mozzarella or stringy cheese, if using, then spoon over the sweet potato stew. Sprinkle on chilli slices and coriander leaves – fresh and punchy is the idea here, so don't hold back on the garnish. Serve with lime wedges for squeezing over.

Roast *sweet potato*,
white beans & crispy sage with quick pickled red cabbage

There is something special about serving things quite simply, letting the individual flavours and ingredients stand up for themselves. The creamy beans in their broth help tie everything together. I often cook a big batch ahead of time to eat in different meals during the week. They are better for it and it makes this dish quick to pull together. Using jarred or canned is fine if you are pushed for time, the method below brings them up to speed.

SERVES 4

- 2 onions, roughly diced
- 3 tablespoons extra-virgin olive oil, plus extra to finish
- 5 garlic cloves, roughly sliced
- 2 sprigs of rosemary
- bunch of sage, leaves picked, stalks reserved
- 1 bay leaf
- 250g (9oz) white beans (cannellini, haricot and coco beans are all good), soaked for 6 hours, or 2x400g (14oz) cans
- 1 small red cabbage (around 600g/1lb 5oz)
- sherry vinegar, to taste
- 4 sweet potatoes (about 600g/1lb 5oz)
- 100ml (3½fl oz) neutral oil (such as groundnut or sunflower), plus extra for roasting
- sea salt flakes

1. If using dried beans, fry the onion in the olive oil over medium heat for 12 minutes until starting to soften. Add the garlic, rosemary, sage stalks and bay. Follow with the beans and enough water to cover. Bring to a simmer and cook for 1–2 hours until tender.

2. If using canned beans, heat the olive oil in a pan, add the onion and garlic and gently soften over medium heat for 12–15 minutes. Add the rosemary, sage stalks and bay leaf, then the beans with their liquid. Heat through for 2 minutes, turn off the heat and set aside to infuse.

3. Finely shred the cabbage. Place in a bowl, sprinkle in some salt and a decent glug of vinegar. Turn over the cabbage to combine everything and set aside.

4. Preheat the oven to 220°C (425°F), Gas Mark 7. When the beans are approaching the finish line, wash the sweet potatoes, cut into 2.5cm- (1-inch) thick slices, lay on a couple of baking trays and coat with around 4 tablespoons of neutral oil and a sprinkle of salt. Roast in the oven for 20 minutes, then turn them over and roast for a further 15 minutes, or until golden on each side and giving to the touch.

5. Meanwhile, heat the neutral oil in a frying pan over a medium heat. In batches, carefully add the sage leaves in a single layer; you don't want to overcrowd them. Cook for 2 minutes, turning once, until they stop bubbling, which means the moisture has evaporated. Remove and drain on some kitchen paper, not too clustered together, to soak up any excess oil and help crisp them.

6. To serve, spoon the beans onto a platter or individual plates. Top with the sweet potato and the sage leaves. Toss the red cabbage, taste a bit to check the seasoning and adjust accordingly. Serve alongside the sweet potato and beans and a drizzle of olive oil.

Potato boulangère

I used to make this with the potatoes cut into slices and all laid out flat, which works just fine. But standing the potato slices up gives a brilliant crunchy element on top, while the bottom half steams and softens, going wonderfully creamy. When slicing the potato, a mandolin is great but by hand is fine; what's important is to slice them as evenly as possible.

SERVES 6

- 150g (5½oz) unsalted butter
- 3 onions, finely sliced
- 4 garlic cloves, finely sliced
- 3 thyme sprigs, leaves picked
- 1.25kg (2lb 12oz) floury potatoes, such as Maris Piper or Desirée, peeled and finely sliced
- 300ml (10fl oz) vegetable stock
- sea salt flakes and black pepper

1. Preheat the oven to 180°C (350°F), Gas Mark 4.

2. Melt half the butter in a large pan that will hold all of the ingredients over medium heat and add the onions, garlic and thyme leaves. Cook gently for 5 minutes. Remove from the heat and stir in the potato slices to coat well with the buttery onions. Season well with salt and pepper.

3. In a 30 × 20cm (12 × 8 inch) baking dish, roughly stack the potatoes upright along the length of the dish. Their edges should point upwards like a roughly shuffled pack of cards and they should sit snuggly. Pour over the vegetable stock and dot the remaining butter evenly over the top of the potatoes.

4. Roast the potatoes in the oven for 50–60 minutes. As they cook they will become creamy and tender underneath and the top edges will crisp. If browning too much on top, cover loosely with foil until tender.

5. Once done, remove from the oven and allow to sit for a few minutes before serving.

Sweet potato salad with loads of herbs & pink peppercorns

Really fresh and bursting with flavour, this salad is great served with flatbreads to scoop it all up. Or roll it up into wraps. An optional tablespoon of tahini in the sauce can add an interesting note, but the pink peppercorns really set everything alight. A rather underrated spice that is so fruity, pink peppercorns should be used much more. They are lovely lightly toasted and crushed, and added on top of curries, soups and stews.

SERVES 4

- 6 sweet potatoes about 1kg (2lb 4oz)
- 1 garlic clove
- 250g (9oz) yoghurt
- 2 tablespoons extra-virgin olive oil, plus extra to serve
- ½ cucumber, deseeded and cut into 1cm (½ inch) cubes
- 1 heaped teaspoon sumac
- 1 tablespoon pink peppercorns, lightly toasted in a dry pan, then roughly crushed in a pestle and mortar
- 15g (½oz) fresh coriander, leaves picked
- 15g (½oz) mint, leaves picked
- 15g (½oz) dill, leaves picked
- sea salt flakes

1. Preheat the oven to 200°C (400°F), Gas Mark 6.

2. Place the whole sweet potatoes on a tray and roast in the oven for 25–35 minutes until completely soft. Remove from the oven and leave to cool slightly until you are ready to serve.

3. Meanwhile, crush the garlic to a paste with a pinch of salt in a pestle and mortar or grate on a fine grater. Transfer to a bowl and mix in the yoghurt and olive oil with a pinch of salt.

4. When you are ready to serve, halve the sweet potatoes and then cut each half into thirds. Spoon the yoghurt sauce onto a platter or serving plate. Follow with the sweet potato, cucumber, sumac and pink peppercorns. Finally mix together and scatter over the herbs. Drizzle with oil and serve.

Potato salad with green beans & toasted buckwheat

This is a joy to eat: lightly dressed potatoes and bright, just-cooked green beans. The buckwheat's crunch adds a different dimension. If you don't have the celery leaves, a finely sliced, tender celery stick works just as well. So does a handful of parsley leaves. Leftover vinegar can be used for salad dressings, when needed.

SERVES 4 AS SIDE OR 3 AS A LIGHT LUNCH

- 225g (8oz) green beans
- 800g (1lb 12oz) new potatoes, scrubbed
- 50ml (2fl oz) red wine vinegar (other vinegars are also fine)
- 2 small onions or banana shallots, finely sliced
- 25g (1oz) buckwheat
- 100g (3½oz) mayonnaise, or use the aioli on page 133
- 10g (¼oz) chives, finely chopped
- sea salt flakes and black pepper

TO SERVE
- leaves from 1 head of celery, 1 finely sliced stick of celery or a handful of parsley leaves
- extra-virgin olive oil, for drizzling

1. Bring a large pan of salted water to a boil.

2. Place the vinegar and onions or shallots in a bowl with a pinch of salt and toss well to combine. Set aside.

3. Boil the green beans in salted boiling water for 3–5 minutes until just tender. Drain from the water with a slotted spoon, as you can use the water for the potatoes later. Refresh the beans under cold water to stop them cooking further.

4. Add the potatoes to the water previously used to boil the green beans and gently simmer for 10–15 minutes until tender when pierced with a knife. Drain and run under cold water until they are room temperature. Drain again. They are good warm but can be chilled further and kept in the refrigerator until ready to assemble and serve; just remove them an hour or so before to lose the chill. You can do the same with the green beans.

5. In a small frying pan, gently toast the buckwheat over medium heat for a couple of minutes until fragrant. Eat one to check if it's done: it should be crunchy. Transfer to a bowl to stop them cooking further and set aside.

6. In a large mixing bowl, combine the potatoes and green beans with the mayonnaise and the chives. Drain the sliced onions and add to the bowl. Add salt and pepper to taste. Arrange on a serving dish or individual plates. Sprinkle over the celery leaves, toasted buckwheat and serve.

Potato & cheddar pie with apple sauce

This pie is a thing of beauty. Layering the cheese means you get molten pockets, which taste really strong against the platform of the potatoes and onions. Do use a strong Cheddar if you can. And eat it warm, just out of the oven; you want it cooled just enough to taste everything but still warm enough that things are still in motion. The apple sauce is a lovely fruity foil. I use whatever variety I have to hand, but go for sharp-flavoured cooking apples if you want something to really cut through the cheese. A good Braeburn or russet is also most welcome. Go for cider over water to add a further dimension.

SERVES 4 GENEROUSLY

FOR THE PASTRY
- 200g (7oz) self-raising flour, plus extra for dusting
- 120g (4¼oz) unsalted butter, very cold, cut into small pieces
- 1 tablespoon cider vinegar or white wine vinegar
- 1–2 tablespoons ice-cold water
- 1 egg, beaten with 1 tablespoon milk
- sea salt flakes

FOR THE FILLING
- 25g (1oz) unsalted butter
- 1 fresh bay leaf
- 2 onions, finely sliced
- 600g (1lb 5oz) potatoes, finely sliced
- 1 heaped tablespoon Dijon mustard
- 200g (7oz) mature Cheddar, coarsely grated

FOR THE SAUCE
- 3 medium apples, cored and diced
- 50ml (2fl oz) water or cider
- mustardy salad, to serve

1. Pulse the flour, butter and a pinch of salt in a food processor until the mix resembles coarse breadcrumbs. Add the vinegar and water. Pulse a couple of times, tip the mix out onto a clean work surface and knead gently to combine. Place in a bowl, cover and chill for 30 minutes.

2. Preheat the oven to 180°C (350°F), Gas Mark 4. Place a baking tray in the oven to heat through. Grease a 24cm (9 inch) or 20–30cm (8–12 inch) square pie dish.

3. For the filling, heat the butter and bay leaf in a pan over a medium heat, add the onions and cook for 10–12 minutes until well softened. Add about 125ml (4fl oz) water, and continue to cook until it has evaporated. Add the potatoes and cook for 1–2 minutes, turning them around to coat well with the onions. Remove from the heat, discard the bay leaf and stir in the mustard.

4. Roll out two-thirds of the pastry to about 5mm (¼ inch) thick and line the base of the pie dish, leaving some overhanging. Roll out the rest of the pastry to form the lid, a little larger than the pie dish.

5. Over the base, lay out a third of the potatoes as flat as possible. Follow with a third of the cheese. Repeat twice. Brush the edges of the pastry with a little of the egg wash and lay the pastry lid on top. Press the two pieces together to seal. Trim the edge to neaten if necessary. Brush with more egg wash and pierce the lid a few times.

6. Place the pie on the heated baking tray and bake in the oven for 40–50 minutes until golden.

7. Meanwhile, in a lidded pan, cook the apples with the water or cider over medium heat for a couple of minutes until the apples are collapsing. Purée with a stick blender until as smooth you like.

8. Remove the pie from the oven and allow to stand for 20–30 minutes. Try to avoid cutting it too soon. Serve with a mustardy salad.

These recipes make more of the humble **CARROT**, which always tends to play a supporting role in a soup or stew. Roasted or steamed in fresh, crunchy salads is where carrots shine. They hold up to being dressed and left in the refrigerator. They are such a great addition to any meal and always readily available.

Quick *carrot* salad

I love this salad. It's a very French way of serving carrots and often appears on my table. Carottes râpées is a simple and refreshing dish that goes with just about anything. Great when piled into sandwiches, it reminds me of trips to France sitting on the roadside eating makeshift picnics. Purple carrots look great but any colour or a mix of colours is fine. With each batch the carrots can taste slightly different, so use more salt or lemon juice as required. A handful of finely chopped parsley is a welcome addition.

SERVES 4 AS A SIDE SALAD

- 3 tablespoons lemon juice
- 1 heaped teaspoon Dijon mustard
- 1 teaspoon honey
- 1 tablespoon olive oil
- sea salt flakes
- 500g (1lb 2oz) carrots, finely sliced and cut into matchsticks, ideally on a mandolin

1. Mix all the ingredients except the carrots in a large mixing bowl. Add the carrots and turn well to coat completely. Allow to stand for at least 15 minutes before serving. Taste and adjust with any element you feel needs more of a presence. The salad keeps well sealed in the refrigerator for a few days.

Roasted *carrots* with chilli flakes, fennel seeds, goat's curd & marjoram

I really love this way of cooking carrots; it intensifies the flavour and is super simple. The crunchy fennel seeds and heat from the chilli work really well with the sweet chewiness of the carrots and the refreshing sharpness of the goat's cheese. Go big on the herbs if you like; it's hard to overdo them. Feel free to use other soft green herbs; basil, coriander, oregano or mint would all be great but most work well.

SERVES 4 AS A SIDE DISH OR 2 AS A LIGHT LUNCH

- 600g (1lb 5oz) carrots, stalks and leaves trimmed
- 3 tablespoons olive oil
- 1 teaspoon chilli flakes
- 2 teaspoons fennel seeds
- 125g (4½oz) goat's curd or soft goat's cheese
- handful of oregano, marjoram leaves or other soft herbs
- 2 tablespoons extra-virgin olive oil
- sea salt flakes

1. Preheat the oven to 200°C (400°F), Gas Mark 6.

2. Toss the carrots in the oil in a baking tray with a liberal pinch of salt. Roast them in the oven for 45–60 minutes, turning occasionally to help get all the sides well cooked, until they are very soft. When they are almost done, or 5 minutes before the end, add the chilli flakes and fennel seeds. Give the tray a shake to roll the carrots in the spices a little and coat with the oil. Once the spices have become aromatic, remove the tray from the oven.

3. Arrange the carrots on a serving plate or platter, trying to leave behind the cooking oil in the tray. Spoon on teaspoon-sized scoops of the goat's curd or break teaspoon-size pieces of the soft goat's cheese over the top. Add the oregano, marjoram or other soft herbs.

4. With the help of a spatula, place the leftover cooking oil and spices from the tray into a mixing bowl. Add the extra virgin olive oil and mix with a pinch of salt if needed. Spoon this over the carrots and serve.

Cumin-spiced *carrot* salad

Really quick to put together, this salad will happily sit alongside many other dishes. It is delicious as part of a Vietnamese noodle salad, alongside falafels or in pitas and wraps to add crunch. I like to make a double batch and put it down on the table at barbecues for guests to help themselves. It goes well with pretty much anything.

SERVES 4 OR 8 AS A SIDE SALAD OR SANDWICHES

- 1 tablespoon cumin seeds
- 1 tablespoon honey
- 2 tablespoons olive oil
- 2 tablespoons cider vinegar
- 400g (14oz) carrots, finely sliced with a vegetable peeler, mandolin or knife
- 20g (¾oz) fresh coriander, leaves picked and stalks finely chopped
- sea salt flakes and black pepper

1. In a small pan slowly dry-toast the cumin seeds over medium-low heat for 3–4 minutes until aromatic, stirring occasionally.

2. Transfer to a pestle and mortar and give them a couple of bashes to crack the seeds. Leave chunks as they provide a good texture to the final salad.

3. Combine the cracked seeds, honey, oil and vinegar in a bowl with a good pinch of salt and pepper. Toss the carrots with the dressing and allow to sit for 15 minutes or so, giving them a turn when you remember. The salad can sit for longer if you want; the carrots will start to slacken and give up their juices to add to the dressing.

4. When ready to serve, mix in the coriander stalks and leaves. Arrange in a serving bowl or on a platter and serve.

Carrot & ginger soup

Feel free to play around with this soup. Think of it as a template that will happily accommodate other elements. I sometimes like to wilt some cavolo nero or kale and serve it on top with the garlic and ginger. Crisping up the garlic and ginger adds texture and a baseline warmth to the dish by flavouring the oil at the start. It's definitely a worthwhile step. Stirring in some cooked chickpeas or white beans at the end wouldn't go amiss either. Play around with what feels good at the time.

SERVES 4

- 4 tablespoons neutral oil, (such as groundnut or sunflower)
- 6 garlic cloves, sliced
- 2 tablespoons peeled and matchstick-sliced fresh root ginger
- 2 onions, roughly chopped
- 500g (1lb 2oz) carrots, cut into medium chunks
- 2 litres (3½ pints) vegetable stock
- 2 tablespoons cider vinegar, or to taste
- sea salt flakes
- extra-virgin olive oil, to serve

1. Heat the oil in a heavy-based saucepan over medium heat. Add the garlic and ginger. Fry gently for 5 minutes or so, until the garlic stops bubbling and begins to turn golden. You are looking to drive out the moisture but not cook them too quickly otherwise they will scorch before becoming crispy. Have your kitchen paper ready for draining.

2. Remove the ginger and garlic with a slotted spoon and drain on kitchen paper. Add the onions to the oil with a pinch of salt. Cook for 12–15 minutes until soft and translucent.

3. Add the carrots and cook for a further 5 minutes, stirring. Follow with the vegetable stock and bring to a simmer. Simmer for 15–20 minutes until the carrots are tender: test with a knife or eat a piece.

4. Depending on your mood the soup can stay chunky or blended. Either way, add half the vinegar and taste, adding more until you reach the vibrancy you like. Season to taste with salt and sprinkle over the crispy garlic and ginger. Finish with a drizzle of extra-virgin olive oil.

Carrot & red lentil soup

Warming and comforting, this dish is really versatile. It is rather speedy to prepare and can be used as a sauce for pasta or rice if you want to bulk it up further. I just love it with some crusty bread and yoghurt. The soup is not a bad dish to prepare on a barbecue or fire while camping. You can skip the initial parsley step and add it chopped at the end if you prefer.

SERVES 4

- 2 tablespoons neutral oil (such as groundnut or sunflower)
- 25g (1oz) parsley, leaves picked
- 2 onions, diced
- 5 carrots (around 250g/9oz), sliced about 1cm (½ inch) thick
- 3 garlic cloves, sliced
- 150g (5½oz) red lentils
- 1 teaspoon cumin seeds, toasted and ground
- 1 litre (1¾ pints) vegetable stock

TO SERVE
- 4 tablespoons yoghurt
- good-quality oil, for drizzling (optional)

1. Heat the neutral oil in a saucepan over medium heat. Add the parsley and cook, stirring constantly, for 1–2 minutes until it stops bubbling. When crisp remove with a slotted spoon and drain on kitchen paper.

2. Add the onions and carrots to the oil. Cook over a medium heat for 7 minutes and then add the garlic. Continue to cook gently for a further 5 minutes. Add the lentils, cumin and stock. Simmer for 15 minutes until the lentils are tender. Top up with water if it gets too dry.

3. Serve the soup in bowls topped with a spoon of yoghurt followed by the parsley. A drizzle of good-quality oil never hurts.

Robust and versatile, **BEETROOT** is a joy to eat. Their striking colour adds to any dish: sliced in salads; thrown into soups or stews; grated, seasoned with vinegar and added to sandwiches. They take time to cook, so stick a big pan on in the morning and let them just tick away until they are ready. The classic pairing with sharp goat's cheese is a mainstay for a reason: anything that balances beetroot's earthy sweetness works so well. They also play well with brambles and red fruits; a handful tossed into a salad with some beetroot works a treat.

Boiled *beetroot* with crème fraîche, green chilli & herbs

As they take a while, I often boil beetroot in the evening or when pottering about at home so I can keep an eye on them. The beetroot will absorb the vinegar when hot, so it really helps to flavour them at this stage. If you dress them when cool, the dressing will sit on the outside. If you can't find baby beetroot, any size will do.

SERVES 4 AS A LIGHT LUNCH OR STARTER

- 2 bunches of baby beetroot (about 800g–1kg/1lb 12oz–2lb 4oz), washed and leaves trimmed
- 3 fresh bay leaves
- 50ml (2fl oz) or a good splash of red wine or fruit vinegar
- 200ml (7fl oz) crème fraîche
- 2 green chillies, finely sliced
- bunch of herbs (dill, mint, tarragon, chervil, chives or a mix), finely chopped
- Good-quality olive oil, for drizzling
- sea salt flakes and black pepper

1. Place the beetroot and bay leaves in a pan. Add 3 pinches of salt. Cover liberally with water, about 6cm (2½ inches) above the surface of the beetroot. Simmer over a medium heat for 1 hour, then check if they are done with a knife. (They will most likely need more time.) Continue simmering, topping up the water as needed, checking every 30 minutes or so – or when you remember – until the beetroot easily falls off the knife when pierced.

2. When the beetroot are done, drain and run under cold water for 1 minute. Transfer back to the pan then fill completely with cold water. Allow to sit until you can handle the beetroot.

3. Slip off the beetroot skins and place the peeled ones in a mixing bowl. Add the red wine or fruit vinegar and give them a toss around. Keep mixing them, continuously coating them to help absorption.

4. When ready to serve, halve the beetroot, or cut smaller if needed. Spoon a good dollop of crème fraîche in the centre of each plate. Place the baby beetroot around the crème fraîche in a ring. Garnish with the chilli slices and the herbs. Add a pinch of salt and a grind of pepper. Spoon over any remaining beetroot and vinegar juices and finish with a small drizzle of olive oil.

Roast *beetroot* with raspberry vinaigrette

This dressing may make more than you need, but it keeps well in the refrigerator and can be used on other dishes or salad leaves. I'd argue it's worth making a double batch to make sure you have it on hand. Fruited vinegars add such a wonderful pop of freshness to dishes, plus the vinegar preserves the colours and freshness of the fruit.

SERVE 4–6 AS A SIDE OR STARTER

- 1kg (2lb 4oz) beetroot, halved, washed and leaves trimmed
- 2 tablespoons olive oil, plus more for drizzling
- 125g (4½oz) raspberries
- 125ml (4fl oz) red wine vinegar
- 1 tablespoon honey
- 30g (1oz) pumpkin seeds
- 10g (¼oz) tarragon, leaves picked
- sea salt flakes

1. Preheat the oven to 180°C (350°F), Gas Mark 4. Line an ovenproof dish with greaseproof paper or foil at least double the length of the dish. Do the same widthways on top of the first layer.

2. Place the beetroot in the dish with a splash of water, the oil and a pinch of salt. Then fold the paper over the beetroot, one side at a time, trying to form a parcel and tucking the ends underneath each other. The aim is to get the parcel as sealed as possible. An extra piece of greaseproof paper or foil over the top won't hurt.

3. Place the tray in the oven and roast for 2 hours, turning the tray halfway through. Carefully peel off the paper or foil to expose the beetroot, then cook for a further 30 minutes uncovered.

4. Meanwhile, mash the raspberries with a fork in a small mixing bowl. Add the vinegar and a pinch of salt and stir well to combine. Let it stand until the beetroot is done.

5. Pass the raspberries through a sieve to remove the seeds. Push the pulp through with the back of a spoon. Stir in the honey and add more salt if needed.

6. In a small frying pan, dry-toast the pumpkin seeds over a medium heat for 5 minutes until golden, constantly turning them in the pan. Some will start to pop: this is fine, just continue until they are golden. Set aside on a plate or bowl to cool until ready to serve.

7. Dress the beetroot in the raspberry vinegar. Place on a serving dish, then scatter over the toasted pumpkin seeds, followed by the tarragon leaves. Finish with a final pinch of salt and a drizzle of oil.

Braised lentils with *beetroot*, spring greens, yoghurt & herbs

I tend to make up a big batch of the lentils, which are good year-round, and then add what I have on hand that day or is in season, such as the garlic yoghurt from the roasted cauliflower and apricot salad recipe (page 60), soft cheese, green sauce, fermented chilli sauce, etc. Really take advantage of the platform to uplift any ingredients that take your fancy: spring greens can be torn and wilted in the lentils; quartered boiled beetroot, roasted squash or leeks can be stirred through; top with hard-boiled eggs; mix through some curry oil and top with fried curry leaves to go down an Indian route; add a can or two of plum tomatoes with the stock and serve with mashed or boiled potatoes. You can't really go wrong with experimentation here; the lentils welcome many a pairing. Use any white wine or cider. I often have leftover bits that happily end up in pots like these; you want something to add a bit of acid to the overall dish.

SERVES 8

FOR THE LENTILS

- 50g (1¾oz) neutral oil (such as groundnut or sunflower)
- 4 carrots, peeled and sliced 1cm (½ inch) thick
- 4 small onions, quartered
- 1 fennel bulb, trimmed and roughly diced
- 3 celery sticks, sliced
- 5 garlic cloves, roughly sliced
- 250ml (9fl oz) white wine or cider
- 500g (1lb 2oz) lentils, rinsed and any obvious stones or husks removed
- sea salt flakes and black pepper

TO SERVE

- 200g (7oz) spring greens, trimmed
- 750g (1lb 10oz) boiled beetroot (about 6), quartered
- 250g (85g/5oz) yoghurt
- large handful of soft herbs, such as dill, parsley, chervil, chopped
- extra-virgin olive oil, for drizzling

1. Heat a large pan big enough to fit everything once cooked over a medium heat. Add the oil, swiftly followed by the carrots, onions, fennel, celery and garlic. Give everything a lively stir to combine and get it evenly coated in oil. Let this mix soften slightly for about 6 minutes, stirring occasionally. Cook the veg further if you prefer, but don't let anything colour too much as you want the end result to be bright without too much caramelization.

2. Add the wine or cider, let the alcohol evaporate for 30 seconds and then add the lentils and enough water to cover.

3. Simmer the lentils for 45 minutes or until they are done (check by trying one). Keep the liquid levels topped up to keep everything moving. Once cooked, season to taste with salt and pepper.

4. Tear the spring greens and wilt into the lentils, stir in the quartered beetroot, top with the yoghurt and chopped herbs, then drizzle with oil to serve.

Beetroot terrine with wholegrain mustard cream

This is a great dinner party dish, which also transports well in the tin if you want to eat it al fresco. It is important to lay the first layer of beetroot slices in a nice pattern for presentation, as they will be on top when the terrine is turned out. The other layers can be arranged a bit more freely, but pay attention to keeping everything relatively even, otherwise the terrine can end up a bit bumpy. Once out of the oven, I give everything a bit of a press down with a tea towel to make sure any bumps or air pockets are evened out. This helps it set together well when cooling. The flavours will develop over a day or so, therefore please do make the terrine ahead of time; it is the better for it.

SERVES 8

- 1kg (2lb 4oz) beetroot, peeled and very finely sliced
- 2 red onions, very finely sliced, preferably on a mandolin
- 2 good sprigs of thyme, leaves picked
- 1 tablespoon olive oil
- 500ml (17fl oz) vegetable stock
- sea salt flakes

TO SERVE
- 250ml (9fl oz) double (heavy) cream
- 3–4 tablespoons wholegrain mustard

1. Preheat the oven to 180°C (350°F), Gas Mark 4. Line a 30 x 12cm (12 x 5 inch) terrine or loaf tin, equally a 20cm (8 inch) round cake tin works well, with baking parchment.

2. In a mixing bowl, toss together the beetroot, onion and thyme leaves with the oil and a couple of pinches of salt.

3. In the terrine or cake tin, evenly layer the beetroot and onions. The better distributed and more evenly packed the mix, the better the end terrine. Try to layer the mix without lumps. Pour over the stock and cover tightly with foil.

4. Place the terrine in the oven and cook for an hour and a half, turning the dish halfway through. Remove the foil and cook for a further 30 minutes. Once the liquid has evaporated, and a knife pierces the terrine easily through the centre, it is done. Remove the terrine from the oven and allow to cool.

5. Push down on the terrine and fold back onto the main body any escaping slices, neatening it up if needed. Place a piece of greaseproof paper on top and use a clean tea towel to gently compress any lumpy areas and removed air pockets. Leave to cool at room temperature and then place in the refrigerator and leave for 2 hours.

6. When you are ready to serve, beat the cream until it starts to thicken. Add the mustard and a pinch of salt. Continue to turn over with a spoon until it thickens further. The cream should not be overly tense: either a spoonable consistency or enough to hold a smooth dollop on the plate.

7. Turn out the terrine onto a board and slice evenly. Place a slice on each plate followed by a dollop of the mustard cream.

SQUASH & PUMPKIN

Where to start? **SQUASH & PUMPKIN** have such a variety of textures, shapes and flavours. I like to keep their integrity, to let them retain their voice in large chunks or big proportions. It's also much easier to cook them in the biggest chunks possible, even whole. When simply roasted until the edges are crisp and the flesh is sweet and tender they're hard to beat. They actually get better by being stored raw in a cold dark place: it improves their flavour and sweetness. Depending on the variety, they can keep up to six months this way.

Roast *butternut squash* with whipped tahini, pickled red onion & mint

This recipe works well with any roasted vegetable really, so feel free to sub in what you have on hand. Some yoghurt stirred through the tahini sauce is a welcome addition.

SERVES 4 AS A SIDE

- 1 butternut squash (around 1.2kg/2lb 10oz), halved, deseeded and cut into rough large chunks
- 3 tablespoons neutral oil (such as groundnut or sunflower)
- 1 red onion, finely sliced
- glug of red wine vinegar
- 200g (7oz) tahini, or more to taste
- squeeze of lemon juice
- handful of mint leaves
- good-quality olive oil, for drizzling
- sea salt flakes and black pepper

1. Preheat the oven to 220°C (425°F), Gas Mark 7. Place the butternut squash in a baking tray with the oil and a healthy pinch of salt, then mix to coat the squash. Roast in the oven for 25–35 minutes, turning once after 15 minutes.

2. Meanwhile, place the red onion in a mixing bowl, separating the slices into strands. Add a pinch of salt and a healthy slug of the red wine vinegar. Mix thoroughly to coat all the onion, then set aside to macerate. Give it a turn whenever you remember to help keep everything moving along.

3. In another mixing bowl add the tahini with 125ml (4fl oz) cold water and a pinch of salt. Stir gently with a whisk at the beginning to start to combine. Once the mix is smooth, check the seasoning, add more salt if needed, then add the lemon juice and stir to combine. Depending on the tahini and your taste you can add more tahini if you want it thicker or more water to loosen it a bit.

4. Once the butternut squash is soft and nicely caramelized, remove from the oven. Spread the tahini sauce on a plate or serving platter. Top with the butternut squash. Drain the onions, which should have a nice vinegary bite and lovely pink colour, then add on top of the squash. Tear over the mint leaves and finish with a flourish of the olive oil and some cracked black pepper.

Pumpkin gnocchi with spinach sauce

A fairly simple and delicious way to showcase these two ingredients, each complementing rather than overpowering the other. The vibrant green, nutrient-rich sauce is a wonderful sea of green. I love making gnocchi, whether potato or pumpkin. Once you've made it a couple of times you get a feeling for it and making it becomes second nature. I like to pull off a piece of the dough and cook it before shaping to test the flour ratio, as all pumpkins are not made equal and some retain more water than others. If the gnocchi floats to the top and holds together then I carry on. If it breaks apart or is too loose, then I knead in another 50g (1¾oz) of flour and try again until it holds together. For the pumpkin, roughly 1kg (2lb 4 oz) raw will result in 400g (14oz) of purée after roasting.

SERVES 4 GENEROUSLY

FOR THE GNOCCHI
- 400g (14oz) mashed, puréed, passed through a ricer flesh of pumpkin or squash. 'Crown Prince', Delica or red kuri work well
- nutmeg, grated to taste
- 1 egg
- 200g (7oz) flour, preferably 00 though plain will do
- sea salt flakes and black pepper

FOR THE SAUCE
- 150g (5½oz) butter
- 250g (9oz) spinach
- 85g (3oz) Parmesan

1. Place the mashed pumpkin on a board. Add the nutmeg and season with salt and pepper. Mix it together with the egg and three-quarters of the flour to form a dough. Don't overwork it; the dough should be soft and light and no longer sticky to the touch. If it is sticky, add a touch more flour.

2. To shape the gnocchi, roll out some of the dough into a rope shape, about 2cm (1 inch) width, then swiftly cut the gnocchi into even pieces along the length of the rope, flicking them away with the end of the knife as each is cut. The gnocchi can be kept in the refrigerator, covered, on a tray until ready to be used later that day.

3. Melt the butter in a high-sided pan over a medium heat. Meanwhile, roughly chop the spinach. Once the butter is foaming, add the spinach with a little salt and stir to combine. Cook for 1–2 minutes until the spinach has wilted. Transfer to a blender and set aside.

4. To cook the gnocchi, bring a large pan of well-salted water to a rolling boil. Drop in the gnocchi (in batches if needed) and cook for 1-2 minutes. When they float to the top, give them a further 30 seconds to ensure they are cooked through. Scoop out, reserving the water, into the pan used for the spinach or a large mixing bowl. Add a ladle, more if needed, of the reserved gnocchi cooking water to the blender with the spinach and blitz to form a sauce. Check the seasoning, then add to the gnocchi. Grate half the Parmesan into the gnocchi and stir together. If the sauce is a too thick, add some more of the reserved cooking water to loosen.

5. Divide between individual plates or place on a serving platter and serve with the remaining Parmesan, and some black pepper. A drizzle of oil wouldn't go amiss either.

Whole roasted *squash* with blue cheese sauce & walnuts

A killer dish to warm the soul. It's almost worth setting yourself in good stead with a bracing hike before eating with a glass or two of wine. Fairly no nonsense to prepare, it is one of those meals where a few people can lend a hand to help make the spätzle. A sharp, slightly acidic cheese is preferable in the sauce: Cashel Blue, Roquefort or Stilton work well. If not making the spatzle, serve with plain rice, grains or pasta.

SERVES 4

– 1 squash or pumpkin, waxy fleshed, such as 'Crown Prince', Delica or red kuri (about 1.2kg/2lb 10oz)

FOR THE BLUE CHEESE SAUCE
– 25g (1oz) unsalted butter
– 1 small onion, finely diced
– 1 garlic clove, finely grated
– 1 tablespoon flour
– 200ml (7fl oz) milk
– 200g (7oz) blue cheese
– sea salt flakes and black pepper
– 100g (3½oz) walnuts, toasted slightly in the oven and broken into chunks, to serve
– a pinch of parsley

FOR THE SPÄTZLE
– 4 eggs
– 120ml (8 tablespoons) milk or water
– 250g (9oz) spelt flour or plain flour
– ¼ teaspoon salt
– 2 tablespoons butter

1. Preheat the oven to 180°C (350°F), Gas Mark 4.

2. Put the squash or pumpkin on a baking sheet and place in the oven. Roast for 45 minutes–60 minutes, turning around halfway, until a knife easily pierces the flesh.

3. Meanwhile, to make the cheese sauce, melt the butter in a saucepan over a medium–low heat. Add the onion and cook for 10 minutes, preferably covered with a lid. You want the onion to be soft and sweet but without colour. Add the garlic and cook, covered, for a further 5 minutes or until everything is very soft. Add a dash of water to help if it sticks.

4. Add the flour and stir well to evenly distribute. Add the milk and stir really well: as the flour cooks out and absorbs the milk it will thicken a lot. Reduce the heat to low and keep stirring for about 5 minutes, until the flour is fully cooked out and the mix coats the back of a wooden spoon or spatula. Remove from the heat.

5. Cut the cheese into rough cubes. While the sauce is still hot, start adding the cheese in four batches. After each addition stir well with a spatula to help the cheese melt into the onion mixture and start to form the finished sauce. Once all the cheese is combined check the seasoning for salt and add some pepper. Set aside until you are ready to serve. The sauce is good at room temperature, but also can be warmed through just before serving. If you want it to be slightly more refined, blend the sauce to get it really smooth.

6. To make the spätzle, bring a large pot of salted

water to a simmer. In a mixing bowl beat the eggs, then add the milk or water, flour and salt and mix well with a fork or whisk to combine.

7. Holding a colander with big holes over the simmering water, push about 6 spoonfuls at a time of the spätzle mixture through the colander into the water. Or drizzle the mixture into the water in a circular motion.

8. Cook the spätzle for 23 minutes, or until they rise to the surface. Allow them to bubble around on the surface for a further minute to cook through. Fish them out with a sieve, drain over the pot, and place them with the butter in a mixing bowl. Give them a toss around to coat in butter. Repeat the process until all the spätzle are cooked and dressed in butter. Check the seasoning and add salt if needed.

9. Spoon the buttered spätzle onto plates or a serving platter. Top with sections of squash, seeds removed. Spoon over the sauce and finish with the walnuts and a sprinkle of parsley.

Butternut squash,
potato & red onion gratin

I like this dish as more of a warmer weather offering. It is less rich and creamy than usual gratins, as I use stock rather than cream. King Edward or Maris Piper potatoes are good to use in this recipe. I use a mandolin to slice the veg so it's all uniform and quick to do. Feel free to just use a knife, but try to get the slices as close to each other in width as possible so everything cooks at the same pace. If you want the rosemary to take less of a main role, then reduce the amount or swap in something else: sage would also be a winner here.

SERVES 8

- 50g (1¾oz) unsalted butter
- 3 red onions, finely sliced
- 5 garlic cloves, finely sliced
- 3 healthy sprigs of rosemary
- 250ml (9fl oz) sherry or oxidized wine (white wine or cider is also fine)
- 1.5kg (3lb 5oz) potatoes, finely sliced
- 1 butternut squash (about 750g–1kg/1lb 10oz–2lb 4oz), finely sliced, deseeded
- 250g (9oz) firm sheep's cheese, grated, or crumbled feta
- 100g (3½oz) Parmesan, grated (Cheddar or other firm cow's cheese is also fine)
- sea salt flakes and black pepper

TO SERVE
- green salad
- bread

1. Preheat the oven to 200°C (400°F), Gas Mark 6.

2. Heat the butter with the sliced onions in a large pan big enough to hold all the ingredients over a medium heat for 8 minutes. Add the garlic and the rosemary and cook for a further 4 minutes, stirring on occasion so nothing catches, until soft. Add the sherry or oxidized wine and boil quickly for 30 seconds to evaporate the alcohol.

3. Add the sliced potatoes and turn several times to get everything coated with the onion mixture. Add the butternut squash, along with 1 litre (1¾ pints) water. Turn everything over and allow to warm through for 3–5 minutes – this will reduce the overall cooking time and get everything going. Add the sheep's cheese and season with salt and pepper.

4. Roughly arrange the vegetables in a suitable baking dish (I use a 36 x 26cm roasting tray), then pour over the pan juices: there will be a fair amount of liquid, but it results in a sort of self-saucing affair once cooked, which helps everything marry together in the finished dish. Top with the Parmesan and bake for 40–60 minutes until easily pierced with a knife and the top is golden.

5. Serve with a green salad and some bread to mop up the juices.

Gratinated roast
pumpkin

More than the sum of its parts, this is a really simple way to bring a meal together. Get really good Cheddar if you can. The other cheese helps add another dimension, but if you don't have it, make up the difference with more Cheddar. I tend to keep a block of hard sheep's or goat's cheese on hand in the refrigerator as it adds a fresh, tangy note to dishes.

SERVES 4 AS PART OF A MEAL

- 1–1.2kg (2lb 4oz–2lb 10oz) Delica pumpkin or other waxy flesh winter squash (such as 'Crown Prince' or red kuri)
- 4 tablespoons neutral oil (such as groundnut or sunflower)
- 150g (5½oz) mature Cheddar
- 50g (1¾oz) hard goat's or sheep's cheese, such as pecorino
- bunch of spring onions, finely sliced, green tips included
- sea salt flakes and black pepper
- 1 lemon, to serve

1. Preheat the oven to 200°C (400°F), Gas Mark 6.

2. Give the pumpkin or squash a rinse under the tap and wipe off any dirt. Cut it in half with a large, sharp knife by putting the pointed end in the top and bringing the knife slowly down to the chopping board, rotating the pumpkin and repeating the other side; the two halves should then separate with a pull. If they don't, cut away any remaining connected parts. Slice into 3–4cm- (1¼–1½inch) wide segments. Cut across these segments at alternating angles to form roughly similar-sized sections.

3. In a mixing bowl, toss the pumpkin sections with the oil and a couple of good pinches of salt until well coated. Place them on a baking tray or two; they shouldn't be too cramped. Roast in the oven for 25 minutes.

4. Remove the trays from the oven and flip the pumpkin pieces over. Turn the trays and return to the oven. Roast for a further 10–15 minutes until golden at the edges and cooked through. Remove from the oven.

5. In a bowl, mix together the cheeses and spring onions with a good pinch of salt and five or so grinds of pepper.

6. Preheat the grill. In a roasting dish, or combined onto one of the baking trays, arrange the pumpkin segments together in a rough tumble, skin-sides down, where possible. Scatter over the cheese mixture and grill for 5–10 minutes until melted. Grate over the lemon zest and serve.

CAULIFLOWER BROCCOLI & OTHER GREENS

CAULIFLOWER can really take the heat and tastes all the better for it. It has is a richness that makes it ideal as the main component of a meal and it welcomes being dressed in sauces and marinades. I like to cook them whole or in the biggest segments possible. If roasting cauliflower, turn the oven up high and throw it in, cooking quickly to ensure a crisp golden exterior and soft, tender, steamed interior.

Spiced *cauliflower* with celery & blue cheese dip

If you can, chill the sauce before serving with the hot cauliflower. Equally both elements work really well piled into buns as sandwiches. Try roasting roughly sliced onions alongside the cauliflower as well.

SERVES 4

- 4 tablespoons neutral oil
- 1 teaspoon paprika
- 1 teaspoon ground cumin
- 1 teaspoon ground coriander
- 1 cauliflower (about 1.3kg/3lb), broken into florets, stalk cut into similar-sized pieces, leaves kept intact
- 250g (9oz) yoghurt
- 150g (5½oz) blue cheese (Cashel Blue or Roquefort)
- 1 garlic clove, crushed to a paste with some salt, or 1 teaspoon garlic granules or powder
- 1 teaspoon mustard (English)
- 1 teaspoon lemon juice, plus more to taste
- 2 celery sticks, diced
- 1 shallot or small onion, very finely diced or finely grated
- bunch of chives, finely sliced
- sea salt flakes

1. Preheat the oven to 220°C (425°F), Gas Mark 7. In a mixing bowl combine the oil with the spices and a good pinch of salt. Add the cauliflower and toss to coat well. Lay out on baking trays so it isn't cramped.

2. Roast the cauliflower in the oven for 12 minutes. Turn it over and cook for a further 8–10 minutes. Once the cauliflower is golden, soft inside and has good caramelization on its edges, remove from the oven.

3. Meanwhile in a blender, pulse the yoghurt, blue cheese, garlic, mustard, lemon juice and a pinch of salt until smooth. Taste and add more salt and lemon to taste. Stir the celery into the cheese sauce along with the shallot and most of the chives.

4. Arrange the cauliflower on a platter and serve the sauce alongside, topped with the remaining chives.

Cauliflower curry
with onion salad

Using cross sections of cauliflower is a lovely way to present this dish, but feel free to just break up the cauliflower into florets, roast, then toss in the sauce and serve as a more traditional curry. Also leaving the cauliflower to absorb the sauce in this way is very beneficial. If serving the cross sections, which does look impressive, tuck any loose roasted bits underneath and place the cauliflower steaks on top. Using two smaller cauliflowers increase the success rate of getting four decent cross sections.

SERVES 4

- 5 garlic cloves, crushed under the heel of a knife
- 100ml (3½fl oz) sunflower oil
- 1 medium onion, diced
- 1 medium carrot, topped and diced
- 1 tablespoon fennel seeds
- 1 heaped tablespoon mild curry powder
- 2 x 400g (14oz) cans whole plum tomatoes
- 1kg (2lb 4oz) cauliflower, stalks and tender leaves included
- sea salt flakes

FOR THE SALAD
- 2 small onions, peeled and finely sliced
- 2 green chillies, finely diced, with seeds if you want the heat
- juice of 2 limes, lemon also works
- 15g (½oz) fresh coriander, leaves picked and chopped, or mint or lemon balm

1. Gently warm the oil in a pan with the garlic. Once the garlic begins to turn golden turn off the heat and set aside to infuse. Preheat the oven to 200°C (400°F) Gas Mark 7.

2. In a medium pan, heat 2 tablespoons of the garlic infused oil and sauté the onion and carrot with a pinch of salt for 12–15 minutes until soft. Then add the fennel seeds and curry powder and toast for a minute. Add the tomatoes, plus the equivalent of one can of water, and simmer for 15–20 minutes until slightly reduced and thickened. Blend until smooth.

3. Cut your cauliflower, complete with leaves attached, into four. Slices work well, though wedges are also fine. Place the cauliflower pieces on a baking tray (sheet) and drizzle with rest of the garlic oil (discarding the garlic). Turn them around in the oil to coat, and sprinkle with sea salt flakes. Roast in the oven for 35 minutes, keeping an eye on it – you want a good caramelization, but it can quickly go too far. That being said, don't fear the heat. Turn the pieces once after 20 minutes.

4. To make the salad, mix the onion with the chilli and lime juice. Season to taste and adjust the lime juice accordingly, then add the chopped coriander.

5. The cauliflower is ready once golden all over. Serve it atop the tomato sauce on a serving plate or platter. With the onion salad on the side. This dish is excellent served with rice and naan bread.

Roast *cauliflower*, garlic yoghurt, walnut & apricot salad

This is a great salad to make any time. It works well as part of a meal or just with rice or flat bread. The sweet apricots complement the spicy garlic and rich cauliflower so well.

SERVES 4 AS PART OF A MEAL

- 2 red onions, sliced 5mm (¼ inch) thick
- 6 tablespoons neutral oil (such as groundnut or sunflower)
- 60g (2¼oz) walnut halves
- 1 cauliflower (about 1kg/2lb 4oz), broken into florets, stalk cut into similar-sized pieces, inner leaves kept intact
- 150g (5½oz) yoghurt
- 1 garlic clove, finely grated or minced, or 1 teaspoon garlic granules
- 1 tablespoon extra-virgin olive oil, plus extra for drizzling
- 100g (3½oz) dried apricots, unsulphured if possible, roughly sliced
- 15g (½oz) parsley, leaves picked
- sea salt flakes

1. Add the onions to a pan with 2 tablespoons of the neutral oil and a pinch of salt. Cook over a medium–low heat for 30–40 minutes until caramelized and jammy. Remove from the heat and set aside until ready to serve.

2. Preheat the oven to 150°C (300°F), Gas Mark 2. Spread the walnuts on an oven tray and roast for about 8–12 minutes until golden. Set aside and increase the oven temperature to 250°C (475°F), Gas Mark 9.

3. Coat the cauliflower in the rest of the neutral oil and a good pinch of salt. Place on an oven tray and roast in the oven for 12 minutes. Turn the pieces of cauliflower and cook for a further 8–10 minutes. Once the cauliflower is golden and has good caramelization remove from the oven.

4. Mix the yoghurt with the garlic, extra-virgin olive oil and salt to taste.

5. In a bowl, toss the cauliflower with the caramelized onions, apricots and half of the parsley.

6. Spoon the yoghurt mixture onto a platter or individual plates. Top with the cauliflower. Add the roasted walnuts and then the remaining parsley. Drizzle with extra-virgin olive oil and add a final pinch of salt.

Cauliflower cheese tart

The pastry here is fairly short because of the walnuts. Don't worry if it cracks when rolling out. Once in the tin, try and patch it up a little with some offcuts. But as the mix is fairly thick it won't run out and stick, so don't worry too much. Make sure to cook the roux to the point where it starts to come away from the sides of the pan. This is when you know it is done. To bake blind I use dried beans but rice also works. Reserve afterwards and reuse for another pastry. I use a 30 × 20cm (12 × 8 inch) rectangular flan tin for this, but a similar-sized baking dish or a 24cm (9 inch) round tart tin works just as well.

SERVES 8

FOR THE PASTRY
- 200g (7oz) wholemeal flour, chilled in the refrigerator, plus extra for dusting
- 100g (3½oz) walnut halves
- 100g (3½oz) unsalted butter, diced and well chilled
- ½ teaspoon sea salt flakes
- 1 tablespoon cider or white wine vinegar

FOR THE CAULIFLOWER CHEESE
- 1 cauliflower (about 1kg/ 2lb 4oz), broken into small florets, stalk and tender leaves cut into similar-sized pieces
- 50g (1¾oz) unsalted butter
- 50g (1¾oz) plain flour
- 500ml (17fl oz) milk
- 2 tablespoons English mustard, or to taste
- a few gratings of nutmeg, or to taste
- 250g (9oz) mature Cheddar grated
- 3 eggs, beaten well
- sea salt flakes and black pepper

TO SERVE
- 2 baby gem lettuce, leaves separated
- lemon juice, to taste
- sea salt flakes and black pepper

1. To make the pastry, put the flour, walnuts, butter and salt in a food processor. Pulse until the mix resembles fine breadcrumbs. Add the vinegar and 2 tablespoons of cold water, then pulse a couple more times to combine. Turn out and bring the mix together into a mass. Cover and let it sit for 15 minutes (an upturned mixing bowl works well).

2. Dust a work surface with flour, place the dough in the middle and sprinkle with some more flour. Roll out the pastry in long strokes going in one direction at a time; avoid rolling back and forth over the pastry. Make sure to roll it out larger than your tin. Place a 30 × 20cm (12 × 8 inch) flan tin (a roasting tray also works fine) underneath and roll the pastry over the tin. Lift the edges to let the pastry fall into the tin, then gently coax it into the edges, trying not to stretch the dough. Tuck over any extra pastry that comes over the edge. Place in the refrigerator to rest for 30–45 minutes.

3. Preheat the oven to 200°C (400°F), Gas Mark 6. Place the flan tin on a baking tray, line the pastry with greaseproof paper and fill with baking beans. Bake in the oven for 20 minutes. Remove the baking beans and cook for a further 10 minutes until golden. Remove from the oven and set aside.

4. Meanwhile, bring a pan of water to a boil and place a colander over the top. Add the cauliflower, cover and steam for 10–15 minutes until tender. Alternatively, boil the cauliflower for 7–10 minutes, but make sure to spread it apart on a baking tray afterwards to allow the moisture to evaporate.

5. To make the sauce, melt the butter in a medium, heavy-based saucepan, add the flour and stir with a whisk to combine well. Cook the roux mix for about 5–8 minutes over a medium–low heat. You want it to become golden for a deeper flavour to the final sauce.

6. Add the milk, 100ml (3½fl oz) at a time, stirring vigorously to completely combine before adding more. When you have added all the milk, gently cook the sauce for 5–10 minutes until it has thickened enough to coat the back of a spoon.

7. Take off the heat. Add the mustard, season with salt and pepper and add the nutmeg to taste. Follow with 200g (7oz) of the cheese. Stir everything to combine and check the seasoning.

8. Reduce the oven temperature to 180°C (350°F), Gas Mark 4.

9. Once the mix has cooled a little, beat in the eggs and then add the cauliflower, making sure to mix well. Spoon this mix into the tart case. Top with the remaining cheese and bake in the oven for 30–45 minutes until golden on top and set.

10. Remove from the oven and allow to cool slightly to help the tart set a little. Serve with the baby gem leaves, seasoned and dressed simply with lemon juice to cut through the richness of the tart.

Quick pickled
cauliflower

This is a handy pickle to have at the ready. Slice it and add to sandwiches or salads, serve with curries or stews to cut the richness or just have it as a side on the table to pick at. Cider vinegar is a bit softer and welcome here, but do experiment with other vinegars you like. The pickle juice can be used to make dressings or added to soups or stews for a bit of pep. These are fridge pickles, so they should be stored cool in the refrigerator. The vinegar level is lower to allow the flavours of the veg to shine through. If you want more kick, up the vinegar amount.

MAKES 8 PORTIONS

- 1 cauliflower (about 1kg/2lb 4oz) broken into small florets, stalk cut into similar-size pieces, tender leaves reserved
- 1 red onion, finely sliced
- 1 small carrot (with skin), washed then finely sliced into rounds
- 1 red or green chilli, sliced
- 3 garlic cloves, finely sliced
- 2 fresh bay leaves
- 1 teaspoon black peppercorns

FOR THE PICKLING LIQUID
- 20g (¾oz) sea salt flakes
- 45g (1½oz) honey
- 450ml (15¼fl oz) cider or white wine vinegar
- 250ml (9fl oz) water

1. Place all the ingredients except for the pickling liquid in a heatproof jar that comfortably fits them all. I use a 2-litre (3½-pint) sterilized jar for this.

2. Measure the pickling liquid ingredients into a pan and set over a high heat to bring to a boil. Boil for 1 minute, then carefully pour into the jar to cover all the veg. Top up with a little boiling water from the kettle if needed.

3. Once cool, store in the fridge.

4. The cauliflower can be eaten after 24 hours, but will improve the longer you leave it. It is at its peak after about a week. Once opened it will keep for a month in the refrigerator.

BROCCOLI is definitely up there as one of the most consumed vegetables in our household. It is so versatile across cuisines and meals: I often use it in an omelette for breakfast or in a noodle salad at lunch or dinner, or I dress it with vinegar, oil and olives to make a quick side salad. It offers a myriad of possibilities and is liked by all as far as I can tell. I never really understood children's authors' fascination with vilifying broccoli. It's brilliant when cooked well.

Roasted *broccoli* with red onion & pine nuts

A wonderful salad that can be thrown together relatively quickly. It is great paired with rice or couscous or stuffed into pittas. All the elements can be prepped ahead of time and assembled as you are ready to serve. It isn't necessary to serve the dish hot: room temperature is totally fine. I love the nuance of the ingredients: there is a rather healthy amount of pine nuts, but the dish works really well with them as a main player. Walnuts or almonds can be used instead, just chop them a bit before mixing in.

SERVES 4 AS PART OF A LIGHT LUNCH

- 700g (1lb 8oz) broccoli, broken into florets, stalks peeled and cut into similar-size pieces
- 6 tablespoons olive oil
- 2 red onions, cut into eighths through the root
- 80g (2¾oz) pine nuts
- 1 tablespoon red wine or sherry vinegar, or more to taste
- 10g (¼oz) parsley, leaves picked
- 10g (¼oz) mint, leaves picked
- 1 teaspoon chilli flakes
- sea salt flakes

1. Preheat the oven to 200°C (400°F), Gas Mark 6.

2. Toss the broccoli in a mixing bowl with 4 tablespoons of the oil and a good pinch of salt until well coated. Tip onto baking trays so the florets aren't too cramped. Roast in the oven for 25 minutes, turning once after 15 minutes.

3. In a large frying or sauté pan, heat the remaining 2 tablespoons of oil over a medium heat, then add the onions and a pinch of salt. Cook gently for 15 minutes, stirring every now and then. The onions should stay plump and begin to caramelize. Towards the end, add the pine nuts and continue to stir until they are evenly golden. Remove from the heat and add the vinegar.

4. Remove the broccoli from the oven, then add to the pan with the onions. Add the parsley and transfer to plates or a serving platter. Scatter over the mint leaves and chilli flakes.

Broccoli & barley
with blue cheese

Crushing the broccoli retains a nice texture in the overall dish. You can grate and stir through the cheese but I like to place it on the table for people to help themselves. Try using different grains, such as spelt. Rice would also work well. As would other cheeses, a strong Cheddar being the front runner. You get the point. It's a good go-to meal using ingredients that tend to be in the cupboard and refrigerator.

SERVES 4

- 2 tablespoons neutral oil (such as groundnut or sunflower)
- 1 onion, very finely diced a similar size to the barley
- 1 leek, trimmed, cleaned and very finely diced a similar size to the barley
- 200g (7oz) barley
- 200ml (7fl oz) white wine (optional)
- 2 litres (3½ pints) water or vegetable stock
- 1 head of broccoli, broken into florets, florets halved, stalk peeled and roughly chopped smaller than the floret halves
- 3 tablespoons lemon juice, or more to taste
- 200g (7oz) Stilton, or other blue cheese
- sea salt flakes and black pepper
- extra-virgin olive oil, to serve

1. Heat the oil in a heavy-based pan large enough to easily hold the fully cooked barley. Add the onion and cook over medium heat for 7 minutes until starting to soften. Add the leek and cook for 3 minutes until soft but not brown; stir the mix often to avoid it catching.

2. Add the barley and stir to coat with the oil and mix with the onion and leek. At this point add the wine, if using, and allow to bubble for 30 seconds.

3. Add 1.5 litres (2½ pints) of the water or stock and place a lid on the pan. Gently simmer for 25–45 minutes depending on how much bite you like in the barley: it's personal preference. I like to cook this ahead and then allow to cool, reheating when ready to eat with some more water or stock. This way the barley tends to be more plump and soft.

4. While the barley is cooking, in a medium-sized pan with a tight-fitting lid add the broccoli and the remaining 500ml (17fl oz) water or stock. Cover and cook for 5 minutes. Check if the broccoli is tender with a knife; if not, replace the lid and continue to cook until just done.

5. Drain the broccoli and return to the pan. Reserve the liquid to top up the barley if needed then roughly mash with a masher. Stir in the lemon juice with a pinch of salt.

6. Once the barley is cooked and you are ready to serve, add the crushed broccoli to the barley. Stir to combine with a decent cracking of black pepper. Stir through the cheese or place on the table. Add a drizzle of olive oil to finish if you like.

Griddled *broccoli*
with almond & garlic sauce

The vinegar-spiked sauce goes so well with the charred broccoli. The sauce can be made ahead of time and kept in the refrigerator. I like to serve the sauce cold with the hot broccoli on top. Slightly toasting the almonds gives them a touch of colour and adds some depth of flavour. Use the best-quality olive oil you have.

SERVES 4

- 75g (2¾oz) whole blanched almonds
- 2 garlic cloves, peeled
- ½ cucumber, peeled and deseeded
- 75g (2¾oz) stale bread, cut into cubes
- 180ml (6fl oz) cold water, or more if needed
- 110ml (3½fl oz) good-quality extra-virgin olive oil, plus extra for drizzling
- 2 tablespoons sherry vinegar, or to taste
- 2 medium or 1 large head of broccoli (around 1kg/2lb 4oz), trimmed and halved or quartered accordingly, stalk peeled of tough skin
- 4 tablespoons neutral oil (such as groundnut or sunflower)
- sea salt flakes
- zest of 1 lemon
- 1 teaspoon pul biber (Aleppo pepper flakes), to serve

1. Preheat the oven to 200°C (400°F), Gas Mark 6.

2. Place the almonds on a baking tray and toast for 7–12 minutes. Don't let them brown too far, but some colour is good. Remove from the oven and allow to cool.

3. Put the almonds along with the garlic, cucumber, bread, water and olive oil into a blender with a decent pinch of salt and half the vinegar. Blend until very smooth. Taste and add more vinegar and salt until you are happy with the balance. Chill, covered, in the refrigerator until ready to serve. It will keep well for a few days. The sauce will thicken a bit in the refrigerator. If you want it thinner or more spreadable, let it down with a touch of water.

4. Heat a griddle pan or iron skillet over a medium heat. Coat the broccoli with the neutral oil and a sprinkle of salt. Place the broccoli halves cut-side down on the griddle pan and grill for 8 minutes until well charred and mostly cooked through. Turn and grill for a further 5 minutes until cooked through; test with a knife. Alternatively, if you feel like an easier ride, you can roast the broccoli in the oven: place on a baking tray and roast for about 20 minutes at 220°C (425°F), Gas Mark 7.

5. Spoon the sauce onto plates and place a broccoli half on top with a final flourish of olive oil, salt, lemon zest and Aleppo pepper flakes.

Broccoli quiche

My aunt, Glenys, used to always make this whenever I'd be stopping over. It's an old classic that just works so well. Not using cream makes it slightly healthier, as well as a bit more store-cupboard/refrigerator friendly. Feel free to use whatever flour you like; I really enjoy the nuttiness of a coarsely ground wholemeal flour here.

SERVES 6

FOR THE PASTRY
- 250g (9oz) wholemeal flour, chilled in the refrigerator, plus extra for dusting
- 125g (4½oz) unsalted butter, diced and well chilled
- ½ teaspoon sea salt flakes
- 1 tablespoon cider or white wine vinegar

FOR THE FILLING
- 1 tablespoon unsalted butter
- 1 onion, finely diced
- 6 eggs
- 175ml (6oz) milk
- 1 large head of broccoli (roughly 500g/1lb 2oz), broken into florets and stalk cut into similar size pieces
- 125g (4½oz) mature Cheddar cheese, grated
- sea salt flakes and black pepper

1. To make the pastry, put the flour, butter and salt in a food processor. Pulse until the mix resembles fine breadcrumbs. Add the vinegar and 2 tablespoons cold water, then pulse a couple more times to combine. Turn out and bring the mix together into a mass. Cover and let it sit for 15 minutes.

2. Dust a work surface with flour, place the dough in the middle and sprinkle with some more flour. Roll out the pastry in long strokes going in one direction at a time; avoid rolling back and forth over the pastry. The diameter of the dough should be roughly 30cm (12 inches). Roll the pastry onto the rolling pin. Place a 24cm- (9½ inches-) deep tart tin underneath and roll the pastry over the tin. Lift the edges to let the pastry fall into the tin, then gently coax it into the edges, trying not to stretch the dough. Tuck over any extra pastry that comes over the edge. Place in the refrigerator to rest for 30–45 minutes.

3. Preheat the oven to 200°C (400°F), Gas Mark 6. Line the pastry with greaseproof paper and fill with baking beans. Bake in the oven for 15 minutes. Remove the paper and beans and cook for a further 10 minutes until golden. Then remove from the oven and set aside.

4. Meanwhile in a large sauté pan or high-sided frying pan melt the butter. Add the onion and cook gently over a medium heat for 12–15 minutes until soft and beginning to colour.

5. In a medium bowl whisk together the eggs and milk. Add the onion, broccoli and cheese with some salt and pepper. Stir to combine and pour into the tart case.

6. Bake in the oven for 35–45 minutes until the centre of the quiche is just set. Serve warm or at room temperature.

Broccoli, spicy tomato sauce & black olives

This dish packs quite a punch. The fiery chilli, sharp onions and briny olives all work together to add complexity. The sauce is deliberately well seasoned to bring everything together. It is well placed as part of a larger meal, or eaten with a grain or couscous to complete the dish.

SERVES 4 AS PART OF A MEAL

- 1 small onion, very finely sliced
- 1 tablespoon red wine vinegar
- 1 tablespoon extra-virgin olive oil, plus extra for drizzling
- 3 tablespoons olive oil
- 3 garlic cloves, finely sliced
- 1 heaped teaspoon chilli flakes, or to taste
- 400g (14oz) can whole plum tomatoes
- 150g (5½oz) Kalamata olives, torn in half and pitted
- 15g (½oz) parsley, leaves picked
- 700g (1lb 8oz) broccoli, divided into florets, stalk peeled and cut into similar-size pieces
- sea salt flakes

1. In a large mixing bowl combine the onion, vinegar, extra-virgin olive oil and a good pinch of salt. Give the onion a good stir to incorporate well.

2. Heat the olive oil in a pan over a medium heat. Once hot add the garlic, sizzle for 1 minute, follow with the chilli flakes for 30 seconds and then add the tomatoes. Roughly break up the tomatoes with a wooden spoon (I like to use a masher). Fill a third of the can with water and add this to the pan. Bubble away to reduce and thicken slightly for about 15 minutes until it is no longer watery but is still saucy. Taste and adjust the seasoning

3. Add the olive halves to the onion mixture, then follow with the parsley.

4. Blanch the broccoli in well-salted boiling water for about 2–3 minutes until tender. Drain well and add to the onion and olives. Toss well to combine, but try not to break up the broccoli too much.

5. Spoon the tomato sauce onto a platter. Top with the broccoli and spoon over any bits left in the mixing bowl. Drizzle with some extra-virgin olive oil to finish.

Charred *broccoli* with chilli buttered almonds

Buttery chilli-roasted nuts dressed broccoli. I mean, it sounds as good as it tastes. The crunchy almonds and well-cooked broccoli are a perfect match. It's great put down on the table as part of a meal, or equally served as a main. I like to eat this with plain boiled rice, not very heavily seasoned, as all the flavour and punch come from the buttered almonds. It is also really quick to bring together if you are pressed for time.

SERVES 4 AS A LIGHT LUNCH

- 3 small or 2 medium heads of broccoli (around 700g/1lb 8oz)
- 4 tablespoons neutral oil (such as groundnut or sunflower)
- 125g (4½oz) unsalted butter
- 80g (2¾oz) whole almonds (with skins), chopped lengthways into thirds
- 15g (½oz) parsley, roughly chopped
- 1 heaped teaspoon chilli flakes, or to taste (optional)
- sea salt flakes
- boiled rice (optional, if serving as a main)

1. Trim about 2–3cm (¾–1¼ inches) off the tough woody end of the stalks and quarter the broccoli heads through the stalks. Heat the oil in a large frying or sauté pan with a lid (or use a baking tray to cover). Place the broccoli, cut-side down, in the pan and sprinkle in a good pinch of salt. Cover and cook for 5 minutes over a medium–high heat. Alternatively, roast the broccoli in the oven. Place on a baking tray and roast for 10–15 minutes at 220°C (425°F), Gas Mark 7.

2. When the broccoli has started to brown, turn on the other cut side and cook, covered, for a further 5 minutes or so.

3. Turn on the final floret side and cook, covered, for a further 5 minutes. A knife should easily pierce the stalks at this stage. If not, keep cooking, rotating the sides until done. Remove the broccoli and set aside.

4. Wipe any excess oil from the pan with kitchen paper. Melt the butter in the pan until foaming. Add the almonds and cook, continuously stirring, over medium heat for 5 minutes until golden. Add the parsley and chilli flakes and cook for 1 minute, stirring constantly. Remove from the heat. Add a good sprinkle of salt flakes.

5. You can cut each broccoli segment into three or four smaller chunks or leave as they are. Place in a bowl and spoon over most of the almond mix. Toss to coat well. Place on a platter and finish with the remaining buttery almond mix.

GREENS OR CABBAGES of some sort tend to be found in most of my meals. Whether puréed into sauces, roughly chopped or kept whole, they are such life-giving ingredients. A lot of the time, I like to eat greens raw and dressed with lemon juice or just cooked through. Often I just stir in chopped leaves to wilt in a sauce or risotto as a final addition; that way they keep their vibrancy. That being said, they also respond well to being cooked at high heats, crisping the edges and steaming them internally.

Shaved *Brussels sprouts* with Parmesan, roasted pecans, white pepper & lemon juice

In the winter months this bright crunchy salad is a most welcome burst of freshness. It is great alongside other dishes or as a part of a light lunch. I like the flavour that white pepper brings to this dish. But please use black pepper instead. Try swapping in blue cheeses – Roquefort works so well!

SERVES 4 AS A STARTER OR SIDE

- 50g (1¾oz) pecan halves
- 500g (1lb 2oz) Brussels sprouts
- 4 tablespoons extra-virgin olive oil
- juice of 1 lemon
- 100g (3½oz) Parmesan or similar
- sea salt flakes and white pepper (black pepper is also fine)

1. Preheat the oven to 180°C (350°F), Gas Mark 4. Place the pecans on a tray and toast in the oven for 8–12 minutes until golden. Give them a shake halfway through and spin the tray around. Set aside and allow to cool to room temperature.

2. To peel the outer layer from the Brussels sprouts, cut a 5mm (¼ inch) sliver off of the root. This should let the outer leaves fall free. Discard the trimmings.

3. Either with a sharp knife or on a mandolin, finely shred the Brussels sprouts.

4. Place the Brussels sprouts in a large mixing bowl, add 2 tablespoons of the olive oil, a pinch of salt, a few grinds of pepper and the lemon juice. Mix well to combine. Roughly break up the toasted pecans and add. With a veg peeler, shave the majority of the Parmesan into the bowl. Stir again to mix well.

5. Spoon onto a serving platter, into a bowl or on individual plates. Shave over the rest of the Parmesan, drizzle with the remaining oil and serve.

Savoy *cabbage* gratin

The beautiful golden crust on top with crispy cabbage edges hides a creamy, cheesy, mustard-spiked sauce below. The cabbage goes wonderfully with the chestnuts and makes this a great wintertime dish. The richness is kept in check by the acidity from the mustard and this, combined with the wine, makes for a rather alpine-style eating experience. It is important with this recipe to use good-quality wine as it shines through in the finished dish; a dry or oxidative white wine is best.

SERVES 4

- 1 Savoy cabbage (about 800g/ 1lb 12oz), trimmed of any tough leaves and the dry base, cut through the stem into eight wedges
- 2 tablespoons olive oil
- 50g (1¾oz) unsalted butter
- 4 onions (about 600g/1lb 5oz), roughly diced
- 4 garlic cloves, roughly chopped
- 100ml (3½fl oz) good-quality white wine or sherry
- 200g (7oz) crème fraîche
- 1 tablespoon Dijon mustard
- 100g (3½oz) cheese, grated (such as Gruyère or Comté)
- 200g (7oz) cooked chestnuts, roughly broken up
- sea salt flakes and black pepper

1. Preheat the oven to 180°C (350°F), Gas Mark 4.

2. Place the cabbage wedges on a roasting tray, drizzle with the oil and season with salt. Roast in the oven for about 45 minutes until tender and the edges are beginning to colour.

3. Meanwhile, melt the butter in a medium saucepan with a lid over a medium heat. Add the onion, garlic and salt. Cook, covered, for 15–20 minutes until soft but without colour, checking occasionally and giving everything a good stir.

4. Add the wine or sherry and allow to bubble off, stirring, for 2 minutes.

5. Put the mixture in a blender and add the crème fraîche, mustard and half the cheese. Blend until smooth, check the seasoning and adjust accordingly.

6. Spoon some of this sauce onto a suitable dish for the gratin. Add the cabbage wedges, cut-side down, in one layer. Scatter over the chestnut pieces. Coat everything well with the rest of the sauce. Finish with the remaining cheese. Bake in the oven for 30–40 minutes until the sauce is bubbling and slightly thickened.

7. Heat the grill to a high heat. Grill for a final 5–10 minutes to get the top lovely and golden.

8. Crack over black pepper and serve with a salad, to drag around in the gratin juices.

Roast *purple cabbage*
with walnut & smoked cheese sauce

Roasting cabbage gives you really crispy caramelized edges and soft juicy flesh. It is very simple and can then be dressed as you please. Even just a dash of good-quality vinegar is enough. This sauce is silky and creamy, with a subtle smokiness from the cheese. It goes extremely well with the cabbage here, but please do make it separately and have with other things. It is great with greens such as broccoli or steamed leeks. If you can't get smoked cheese, using other semi-soft goat's or sheep's cheese works just as well.

SERVES 4

- 200g (7oz) walnuts (almonds are also fine)
- 1 fat garlic clove, grated
- 120g (4¼oz) best-quality extra-virgin olive oil, plus extra for drizzling
- 250ml (9fl oz) cold water, or more if needed
- 1 teaspoon white wine vinegar, or more to taste
- 60–100g (2¼–3 ½oz) smoked goat's cheese, cubed
- 1kg (2lb 4oz) purple cabbage
- 4 tablespoons olive oil, for roasting
- sea salt flakes

1. Preheat the oven to 220°C (425°F), Gas Mark 7.

2. Place the walnuts in a bowl, pour boiling water over them and leave to soak for 20 minutes. This helps to get rid of any bitterness.

3. Drain the walnuts, place them in a tall container along with the garlic and oil and blitz with a hand blender. Add half the water and blitz some more. Then add the rest of the water along with a decent pinch of salt and the vinegar. Blend until very smooth. Add 60g (2¼oz) of the cheese and blend once again. Taste and add more cheese, vinegar and salt until you are happy with the balance. Chill, covered, in the refrigerator until ready to serve. The sauce will thicken in the refrigerator and will happily keep for a few days.

4. Cut the cabbage into eight wedges, or quarters if using smaller cabbages. Drizzle with oil, sprinkle with salt and then place on a baking tray. Roast in the oven for 40–60 minutes until well charred on the outside and soft inside. Turn once two-thirds of the way through.

5. Spoon the sauce onto a plate or a platter, then top with the cabbage and a final drizzle of olive oil.

Curried lentil & *spring green* hand pies with green chilli

These are handy for picnics, in packed lunches or as a part of a meal. They benefit from the cucumber yoghurt – the freshness and zing cut through the meatiness of the pies and temper the heat from the chillies, so pairing it with them is definitely worth it. If you don't have spring greens, any dark greens work, spinach or Brussels tops for example.

MAKES 8 PIES

- 2 tablespoons neutral oil (such as groundnut or sunflower)
- 1 onion, finely diced
- 3 garlic cloves, sliced
- 1 tablespoon curry powder
- 250g (9oz) lentils, checked for any rogue stones
- 200g (7oz) spring greens, tough stalks removed and leaves shredded
- 2 green chillies, diced
- 2 packets pre-rolled puff pastry (each about 325g/11½oz)
- 2 eggs, beaten
- a pinch of sea salt flakes

FOR THE YOGHURT
- 300g (10½oz) yoghurt
- 1 cucumber, coarsely grated
- 3 tablespoons lemon or lime juice
- a pinch of sea salt flakes

1. Heat the oil in a medium saucepan over a medium heat, then add the onion and salt. Cook for 12–15 minutes until the onion is soft. Add the garlic and curry powder and stir while cooking for a further minute.

2. Follow with the lentils and 1 litre (1¾ pints) of water. Gently cook for about 20 minutes until just tender. Keep topping up with water if needed to keep everything loose, but don't let it get too watery as the mix needs to bind together to fill the pies.

3. Add the leaves to the lentils to wilt. Increase the heat to high to cook off any excess water with a swift boil but take care not to overcook the lentils. It's best to flirt with the level of liquid, erring on the drier side. Stir through the chilli and allow the mix to cool.

4. Preheat the oven to 200°C (400°F), Gas Mark 6.

5. Unravel the pre-rolled pastry sheets. (If using a pastry block, roll out to 40 × 25cm/16 × 10 inches.) Cut each pastry sheet into four rectangles. Spoon a heaped dessertspoon of lentils onto one end of each pastry rectangle. Brush around the edges with egg wash and fold over each rectangle to cover the lentils. Crimp together the edges. I press them down with the end of a fork.

6. Place the pies onto a lightly oiled baking sheet. Brush with more egg wash, then poke a little hole or two in the top of each. Bake in the oven for 20–30 minutes until the pies are puffed and golden. Turn the tray around two-thirds of the way through.

7. Mix the yoghurt ingredients together and serve alongside. Add more lemon to taste.

Ginger & peanut butter roasted *kale*

These crispy kale leaves are very easy and addictively moreish. I eat them on top of rice and noodle salads or simply on their own as a snack. The peanut mixture is so delicious that when I make them with my son we generally eat half the dressed leaves before they make it to the oven. That being said the dressed leaves work well as a salad, so by all means eat them that way as well.

SERVES 4 AS A SIDE OR MORE AS A SNACK

- 500g (1lb 2 oz) kale, green, purple or a mixture, tough stalk ends removed
- 160g (5¾oz) crunchy peanut butter
- 30g (1oz) sunflower oil
- 20g (¾oz) cider vinegar
- 20g (¾oz) soy sauce
- large thumb-sized piece of ginger, peeled and finely grated
- sea salt flakes

1. Heat the oven to 180°C (350°F), Gas Mark 4. Mix all the ingredients, except the kale, in a large bowl (I place the mixing bowl on scales and weigh the sauce ingredients directly). Loosen the mixture with water until it's a pouring consistency.

2. Either lay the kale on baking sheets, making sure they are not overlapping, and drizzle over the sauce, or add the kale to the mixing bowl, toss to combine and then lay on the sheets. Either way the kale wants to be well and evenly coated. I tend to get my hands in and give it a good massage.

3. Roast the kale for 20–30 minutes until crisp, in batches if easier. Turn once halfway through cooking. Depending on the size and thickness of the kale they may take longer.

4. Taste one and add a sprinkle of salt if needed. If not eating straight away, store in an airtight container for a few days.

PEAS are such a wonderful vegetable eaten fresh and tender. Sadly, their flavour dissipates rather quickly, which is why they are the undisputed stars of the frozen food aisle. I have them fresh a couple of weeks in the year but mostly straight from the freezer, as they are so sweet and always on hand. Often I opt for the smaller petit pois, when buying frozen, as they are the most tender.

Chilled *pea* soup

This soup can be quickly made and set to chill in the fridge in the blender jug. That way, you just need to give a little stir and pour directly into bowls. It also works well served in small glasses as a canapé or as an intro to a larger meal or barbecue, as it can be prepped well ahead of guests arriving. I prefer to use petit pois since standard peas can be a little floury, especially if they have been picked a bit later in the season. If you only have the latter, make sure to run the blender for a good few minutes to break them down fully.

SERVES 4

- 2 tablespoons neutral oil (such as groundnut or sunflower)
- 1 onion, diced
- 1 small stick of celery, diced
- 1 garlic clove, roughly chopped
- 500g (1lb 2oz) frozen peas, preferably petit pois
- 3 tablespoons yoghurt
- squeeze of lemon juice, to taste
- handful of soft green herbs (such as chives, mint or chervil)
- sea salt flakes and black pepper

TO SERVE (OPTIONAL)

- finely chopped soft herbs (such as chives, mint or chervil)
- olive or herb oil
- cracked black pepper

1. Heat the oil in a pan over a medium heat. Add the onion, celery and garlic. Cook until completely softened, 12–15 minutes should get you there but go a little longer if needed. If the mixture starts to catch, add a splash of water whenever necessary, you don't want it to colour much. If adding water, try to evaporate any excess before the blending step.

2. Tip the peas into a large mixing bowl and pour over a full kettle's worth of boiling water, about 1.5 litres (2½ pints). Leave the peas to defrost to have the edge taken off their rawness, 2 minutes should do it. If using frozen garden peas rather than petit pois, drain the first round of boiling water and repeat it. After 2 minutes, drain the peas and refresh in cold water.

3. When the onion mixture is ready, drain the peas and put in a blender. Add the onion mixture, along with 500ml (17fl oz) cold water, a decent pinch of salt, the yoghurt and a squeeze of lemon juice. Blitz until smooth, then blitz some more. Try to get the soup as smooth as possible. Feel free to blitz in some soft green herbs if you're feeling jazzy.

4. Taste and balance out any flavours you want more of. Season generously with salt as it will be chilled so will need more to be properly seasoned. Then leave covered for 2 hours in the fridge to chill sufficiently. Top how you would like, with soft herbs, olive oil, herb oil and/or decent amounts of cracked black pepper. Eat with hot toast and cold butter.

Peas & broad beans with lemon & olive oil on feta

I first made this when my brother came to visit as an intro to dinner while we waited for others to gather and our hunger was beginning to grow. Great for snacking on pre meal, or just putting on the table for people to help themselves to as a starter. It can also be all blitzed together in a food processor and used as a pasta sauce let down with some pasta water, or as a spread for toast or crispbread. But I rather like seeing and tasting the individual elements. Another option is to crumble the cheese underneath to help incorporate it and make it a spoonable dish at the table. Use the flatbread recipe from page 103; simply roll out and bake without any toppings.

SERVES 4 AS A STARTER, MORE AS A PRE-MEAL SNACK

- 350g (12oz) fresh broad beans, podded, or 100g (3½oz) frozen
- 350g (12oz) fresh peas, podded, or 150g (5½oz) frozen
- 1 lemon
- 7g fresh oregano, leaves picked, or other soft herbs, dill, basil, tarragon, chervil are all good
- 1 teaspoon pul beber (Aleppo pepper flakes), though other sweet or spicy chilli flakes will do
- good-quality extra-virgin olive oil, to taste
- 400g (14oz) feta cheese
- sea salt flakes

1. In a deep pan of salted boiling water blanch the broad beans until tender. Pluck one out and carefully try, 1–2 minutes should be sufficient. Remove the beans with a slotted spoon and refresh under cold water. Meanwhile drop in the peas for a minute to take the edge off their rawness. Drain and refresh under cold water and put in a separate bowl.

2. Remove the broad beans from their skins, leaving just the bright green inner part. I eat the skins while I'm doing this, but they can also be chopped and added to soups or stews or composted.

3. Add the broad beans to the bowl of peas, along with the zest of half the lemon, a good slug of the oil and most of the herbs. Stir everything with a decent pinch of salt and the juice of half the lemon. Taste and adjust the salt, lemon juice and oil accordingly.

4. Spoon the mixture onto the feta, which has been cut into 1cm (½ inch) slice and finish with the pul beber and the rest of the herb leaves. Spoon onto bread or crackers.

ONIONS & LEEKS

ONIONS & LEEKS The onion family is my favourite set of vegetables, onions in particular, mainly for the seemingly never-ending possibilities but also because they keep so well in the refrigerator or cupboard. They are there supporting so many dishes, providing the base that meals are built upon. But equally they can be centre stage, holding their own. They go so well with fats and acids that a quick meal can be made out of fairly humble, mainstay ingredients.

Steamed *leeks* in a honey & mustard vinaigrette with capers

This recipe is quite simple but clever. This way of serving leeks works alongside other elements on the table or as a starter with the vinaigrette working its way inside the leeks, a trick I learned from Simon Hopkinson. It will sit well, marinating, ahead of being served if you would like to make it in advance. Crusty bread, boiled eggs, mayonnaise and peppery salad leaves complete the lunch scenario, if you desire.

SERVES 4 AS A SIDE OR STARTER

- 6 leeks, trimmed, cleaned and cut into 3cm (1¼ inch) rounds
- 60g (2¼oz) Dijon mustard
- 60g (2¼oz) honey
- 4 tablespoons cider vinegar
- 4 tablespoons extra-virgin olive oil, or more to taste
- 50g (1¾oz) capers, drained
- sea salt flakes

1. Lay the rounds of leek cut-side down on a plate that will fit in a steamer. Or use multiple plates in a stacking steamer. Steam the leeks until soft in the centre and cooked through. Timings will vary but as a guide it should take 10–15 minutes.

2. While the leeks are steaming make up the dressing. Add the mustard, honey and vinegar to a mixing bowl with a good pinch of salt. Mix well to incorporate the honey. Then add the oil, a tablespoon at a time, and stir to combine. Taste the dressing and add more seasoning if needed. Adjust the level of any element you feel should be more prominent. Stir in the drained capers.

3. When the leeks are done, transfer them to a fresh plate and then spoon the dressing over. Because the leeks are cut and cooked in this way, the dressing will work its way down the sections, seasoning the leeks from the inside. They keep well, sealed in the fridge.

Spelt with steamed *leeks* in a cavolo nero & lemon sauce

I like to think of this as a nutrient-rich risotto. Spelt can take a while to cook, so do persevere. It can have a persistent bit so when you are happy with the texture stop. Equally pearl barley can be used.

SERVES 6

- 300g (10½oz) spelt
- 2 onions, sliced
- 3 tablespoons extra-virgin olive oil, or more to taste, plus extra for drizzling
- 200ml (7fl oz) white wine or cider
- 5 garlic cloves, sliced
- 250g (9oz) cavolo nero leaves, picked and chopped, stalks finely sliced
- 2 tablespoons lemon juice, more to taste
- 12 medium leeks, trimmed and cleaned
- 200g (7oz) hard cheese, such as Lincolnshire Poacher or Cheddar
- salt and black pepper

1. Rinse the spelt and add to a pan with enough lightly salted water to cover it well. Bring to a boil and simmer for 45 minutes, or until the grains are cooked through. By all means cook them longer to get a fluffier end product, if you desire.

2. Meanwhile in a frying pan sauté the onions in the oil over a medium heat for 10 minutes until they have begun to soften. Add the wine or cider followed by 200ml (7fl oz) water and the garlic. Let the liquid reduce to half, then add the chopped cavolo nero. Stir well to combine and cook the cavolo nero evenly for 5-10 minutes. You want it to just cook through but keep its colour, so taste to check.

3. Purée with a stick blender, adding seasoning, lemon juice and olive oil to taste.

4. Meanwhile, cut the leeks so they fit in a steamer. Steam them for about 5–7 minutes until a knife will easily go through their flesh. Allow to cool slightly and then cut into 2cm (¾ inch) chunks. I like to do this on a diagonal.

5. When ready to serve, combine the cavolo nero sauce, spelt and leeks in a pan with a splash of water to loosen the mix. Warm through, checking the seasoning. Portion either individually or on a platter, shave over the cheese and drizzle with oil.

Grilled young *leeks* with sauce Gribiche

This dish brings me so much joy: such a wonderful balance of flavours that welcomes the spring and the potential of eating outside. It is just as delicious as a simple lunch with some crusty bread: I prefer brown but any crusty bread is perfect. This dish reminds me of France and summers spent camping and eating well. Chargrilling the leeks adds a little extra note to the overall dish, but if you desire a swifter dish, omit the grilling. Also, the mayonnaise element can be left out – just grate the hard-boiled eggs instead of chopping, for a healthier option. Equally if young baby leeks aren't available, substitute one leek per person, cut into thirds: just as delicious. Both leeks and the sauce can be made ahead and keep well in the refrigerator until ready to serve. Just bring the leeks out an hour ahead of serving to bring them to room temperature.

SERVES 4 AS A LIGHT LUNCH

- 16–20 firm baby leeks, trimmed and cleaned
- 2 tablespoons capers, or more to taste, chopped through
- 8 cornichons, or more to taste, finely chopped, quartered lengthways, then sliced
- 2 tablespoons finely chopped curly parsley
- 2 tablespoons finely chopped tarragon
  200g (7oz) mayonnaise, good-quality shop-bought or use the recipe on page 166
- 3 hard-boiled eggs, roughly diced
- 1 tablespoon neutral oil (such as groundnut or sunflower)
- salt and black pepper

1. Bring a large pan of well-salted water to a boil. Drop in the leeks and poach them for 5-7 minutes until just done, testing them with a knife. They may take a bit longer to poach but keep in mind that they will get a second warming with the grilling, so some bite is good, but the centres should yield. Refresh in ice water to stop the cooking and drain well.

2. Combine the chopped capers, cornichons, parsley and tarragon with the mayonnaise and season to taste. If omitting the mayonnaise, grate the egg coarsely and then combine the remaining ingredients. Add more of any of the elements if you feel it needs it.

3. Bring a griddle pan to a good heat. Sparingly rub the leeks in oil and grill on both sides for 2 minutes until lightly charred.

4. Spoon the sauce onto individual plates or a serving platter. Top with the leeks and serve.

Roasted *onions*,
sumac & parsley

This is a lovely summer dish to add to the table. It's also great in kebabs, salads or sandwiches – think along the lines of halloumi or feta. It is an excellent addition to barbecue offerings when friends and family are over. Making it ahead of time is fine, otherwise try blackening the onions, with their skins still on, on the barbecue grill, or directly in the coals, rotating them to make sure they cook evenly. I use sumac made from just the berries for added zing and freshness. Look for sumac that is red without black specks; they are the seeds and add nothing.

SERVES 4 AS A SIDE

- 8 onions with skins (about 1kg/2lb 4oz)
- 1 tablespoon good-quality sumac, or more to taste
- 2 tablespoons extra-virgin olive oil
- 1 tablespoon pomegranate molasses
- 25g (1oz) parsley, leaves picked
- sea salt flakes

1. Preheat the oven to 200°C (400°F), Gas Mark 6.

2. Place the onions on a baking tray. Roast in the oven for 45–60 minutes until they are beginning to collapse and are soft in the middle.

3. Remove the onions from the oven. Allow to cool until they are manageable.

4. Trim the root end and peel away the outer two layers to reveal the soft flesh or squeeze out the cooked inner layers. Add the flesh to a mixing bowl and discard the skins.

5. Add the sumac, oil, molasses and parsley leaves to the mixing bowl. Mix well to combine. Season with salt. Taste a segment and add more sumac and salt accordingly.

6. Serve the onions on a serving platter with any juices poured over.

Flatbread with potatoes & *onion* sauce

I often make this sauce to go alongside dishes at the table. It can happily take on many forms: dressing potatoes, on flatbreads or pizzas, with Sunday roasts. It's really easy to make and keeps well in the refrigerator. I often use a couple of spoonfuls to start off cooking a soup or stew as it means you can leapfrog past the initial stages of cooking the onions. Also it works well as a topping on finished soups and stews. Or I guess what I am getting at is: use it liberally wherever you see fit. Depending on what I am pairing it with, I will add different herbs. For a Sunday lunch, I add a handful of sage leaves when there's 5 minutes left of baking. Similarly, I add rosemary when making these flatbreads as it goes well with the potatoes.

MAKES 4 22CM (8½ INCH) FLATBREADS

FOR THE SAUCE – MAKES DOUBLE
- 60g (2¼oz) unsalted butter
- 8 onions, quartered
- lemon juice or cider vinegar, to taste
- sea salt flakes and black pepper

FOR THE FLATBREAD
- 500g (1lb 2oz) flour
- 1 teaspoon fine sea salt
- 1 teaspoon fast action dried yeast
- 1 tablespoon honey or sugar
- 300g new potatoes, very thinly sliced

1. Melt the butter in a heavy-based saucepan with a lid. Add the onion and a good pinch of salt. Cook, covered, over a medium–low heat for 40 minutes, giving the onions a stir occasionally to make sure they don't stick. You aren't looking for any colour, just soft, sweet onion segments. If the pan gets a bit dry, add a splash of water whenever needed. Low heat for a long time is key here.

2. Once the onions are collapsing, remove from the heat. The onions can be served at this stage, if you wish. Just check the seasoning and adjust accordingly. Add a couple of drops of lemon juice. Otherwise transfer the onion to a blender, or use a stick blender in the pan, and blend until smooth. Season to taste.

4. To make the flatbreads, combine the flour, salt and yeast in a mixing bowl. Mix the honey or sugar with 600ml (20fl oz) lukewarm water. Mix with a fork to bring together. If the mixture is too dry add in more water until it comes together easily. Use a stand mixer with a dough hook, if you have one.

5. Turn out onto a board and knead well for a few minutes until a smooth dough is formed. Turn the bowl over to cover the dough on the board for about an hour until doubled in size. If not using straight away, leave sealed to rise slowly in the fridge.

6. Heat the oven to 200°C (400°F), Gas Mark 6. When ready knock back the dough and divide into four. Roll out each piece into rounds about 22cm (8½ inch) in diameter, place on a baking tray then spread two dessert spoons of the onion sauce evenly over the dough. Top with the potato slices and a drizzle of dough. Bake for 20–30 minutes until bubbling, golden and the base is cooked through.

Brown sauce

I love a condiment. Sometimes I build meals
backwards from a craving for a certain flavour. This is
a handy sauce to have on hand in the refrigerator. It's
quite fruity and fragrant but balanced with a vinegary
kick. It's good with breakfast as well as cheese and
biscuits, or in sandwiches. Play around with different
molasses. Date or cherry work very well. Also
swapping 200ml (7fl oz) of the water for cider adds a
further note. I often can't find the last star anise after
cooking, so I just blend it in - it's no problem. Consider
using a muslin bag to help retrieve them if you like.

MAKES ROUGHLY 1½ LITRES (2½ PINTS)

- 2 onions, roughly chopped
- 3 celery sticks, roughly chopped
- 2 apples, cored and roughly chopped
- 7 garlic cloves
- decent thumb-sized piece of fresh
  root ginger, peeled and roughly
  sliced
- 1 red chilli, split down the middle
  from just below the stalk
- 500g (1lb 2oz) pitted dates
- 3 star anise
- ½ heaped teaspoon cinnamon
- 1 teaspoon ground coriander
- 200ml (7fl oz/⅓ pint) cider vinegar,
  plus extra to taste
- 150ml (5fl oz) date molasses
- 600ml (20fl oz) water
- sea salt flakes and black pepper

1. Add all the ingredients to a saucepan. Cover and
bring to a gentle simmer. Cook over a low heat for
30–40 minutes until the celery and onions are soft. If
you want a thicker end sauce, leave the lid off during
cooking for half the time and stir occasionally.

2. Remove from the heat and allow to sit for
20 minutes with the lid on.

3. Fish out the star anise and chilli and discard.
Add the rest of the mixture to a blender with a good
pinch of salt and a few grinds of pepper. Blend until
very smooth. Taste and add more salt and vinegar
accordingly. It will take a decent amount of salt, as
well as more vinegar. Add a touch of boiling water if
you prefer the sauce slightly thinner.

4. Pour the sauce into suitable, sterilized jars
and seal. The residual heat will form a vacuum so
the sauce will remain stable indefinitely. If you are
going to use it within the next few weeks, decant
and store in the refrigerator, where it will continue
to keep for a couple of months or so. The sauce
improves with age.

AUBERGINE & PEPPERS

Oh **AUBERGINE AUBERGINE**, you bloody amazing beast! Taker-on of flavours like no other, fluffy and oh so comforting. So very delicious across so many cuisines. Do try to buy firm specimens. I opt for the longer, more slender ones over the more bulbous, as they contain fewer seeds. Simply roasted or griddled whole, split open and dressed, they make for a wonderful offering to build a meal around. In any form, they never get boring.

Miso *aubergines*

Warm from the oven, these are really fragrant and sticky, but it is no bad thing having some left over at room temperature. The sauce will try to fall off as they cook and burn on the baking tray, so I toss the aubergines in roughly half the sauce to coat well Then I spoon the remaining sauce over them 5 minutes before the end. This way the sauce will be sweet and sticky and not left behind stuck to the tray.

SERVES 4

- 3 tablespoons neutral oil (such as groundnut or sunflower)
- 80g (2¾oz) white miso
- 40ml rice wine vinegar
- 40g (1½oz) honey
- thumb-sized piece of fresh root ginger, peeled and finely grated
- 2 garlic cloves, finely grated
- 3 aubergines, quartered lengthways

TO SERVE
- 50g (1¾oz) sesame seeds, toasted
- 2 red chillies, sliced
- bunch of chives, finely sliced
- plain cooked rice

1. Preheat the oven to 200°C (400°F), Gas Mark 6. In a mixing bowl combine the oil with the rest of the ingredients except the aubergines. Mix well to combine.

2. Toss the aubergines in the mixture to coat them well. Place the aubergine segments cut-side down, evenly spaced apart on a baking tray, reserving about half the sauce in the bowl for later glazing. Place the tray in the oven and cook for 10 minutes.

3. Remove the tray and turn each segment onto the other side. Cook for a further 10 minutes.

4. Flip the segments onto the skin side. Spoon over any remaining sauce onto the aubergines. Cook for a final 5 minutes, or until the aubergines are very tender.

5. Once done, remove from the oven, arrange on a serving platter or in individual bowls and liberally coat with the sesame seeds, sliced chillies and chives. Serve with plain rice.

Roast *aubergine*, tahini & tomato seed dressing

This is my interpretation of a dish that I had in Tel Aviv from the restaurant Port Said. It was served with brioche and eaten sitting outside in the open air. It was one of those great food moments. Happily it translates well here and is simple and fast to bring together. If you are making ahead of time, it is a good idea to sit the peeled and split aubergines in the dressing to absorb the flavour and seasoning. The actual tomato halves can be slow-roasted in the oven to be used another time, eaten as is or diced or blitzed into a sauce. This dish is light but packs a good punch of flavour.

SERVES 4 AS A LIGHT LUNCH WITH BREAD AND A SALAD, OR 8 AS A STARTER

- 6 medium, ripe tomatoes
- 4 aubergines
- 150g (5½oz) tahini
- 100ml (3½fl oz) cold water
- 1 tablespoon lemon juice, or more to taste
- 1 garlic clove, finely grated or minced
- 1 teaspoon sea salt flakes, or more to taste
- 1–2 green chillies, deseeded and finely diced (add some seeds if you like)
- 3 tablespoons extra-virgin olive oil

1. Preheat the oven to 200°C (400°F), Gas Mark 6. Halve the tomatoes across the equator. Squeeze each half into a bowl. You want only the juice and the seeds: the flesh can be used in another dish or sauce.

2. From just below the stalk, run a small sharp knife along the length of each aubergine in four evenly spaced cuts, just piercing the skin. Don't go too deep, as the cuts are just to help remove the skin later on.

3. Place the aubergines on a baking tray and roast in the oven for 30–40 minutes, turning once halfway, until evenly cooked and the flesh is very soft when squeezed.

4. Remove the aubergines from the oven and allow to cool until you can handle them.

5. Whisk the tahini with half the water and the lemon juice, garlic and salt. The mixture will look rough, but add some of the remaining water and it will transform and smooth out as you continue mixing. The sauce should be spreadable, thick enough that it clings. Check the flavour – add more lemon juice and/or salt if needed. Set aside until ready to use. The sauce can be made ahead of time and stored in the refrigerator.

6. Mix the tomato seeds, chilli and olive oil with a pinch of salt to taste.

7. Once the aubergines are cool enough to handle, peel them but do not remove the stalk. Run a knife through the flesh from just below the stalk to the base to split the aubergine in half, using the stalk as an anchor of sorts for the flesh.

8. Dollop 2 dessert spoons of tahini sauce onto a plate and spread with the back of the spoon. Place a peeled aubergine on top and spoon over the tomato seed dressing. These can also be all presented on a platter together to serve from at the table if you like. Serve with warm pitas, brioche or crusty bread as you please, with any excess dressing alongside.

Griddled *aubergine*, garlic yoghurt, roasted cherry tomatoes & brown butter

This dish is made for wiping around the plate with chunks of bread. It is equally delicious to have on top of rice or thick strands of pasta. Salty, fatty, sharp, nutty: all good things, made greater by being grouped together on one plate. It can also happily be served at room temperature, just make sure the butter is hot when you serve it. I like to serve this on a large platter or serving bowl in the centre of the table for people to dig into as they please. This works well as part of a larger meal or as a starter with some bread to mop up the juices.

SERVES 4

- 300g (10½oz) cherry tomatoes on the vine (loose are also fine)
- 5 tablespoons neutral oil (such as groundnut or sunflower)
- 4 aubergines, sliced about 2cm (¾ inch) thick
- 60g (2¼oz) walnuts
- 200g (7oz) yoghurt
- 1 garlic clove, finely grated
- 75g (2¾oz) unsalted butter
- sea salt flakes

1. Preheat the oven to 200°C (400°F), Gas Mark 6. Place the tomatoes on an oven tray and drizzle with 2 tablespoons of the oil. Roast for 5–7 minutes until the tomatoes are blistering. Remove and set aside.

2. Meanwhile, heat a griddle pan over a medium-high heat. Brush the aubergine slices with the remaining oil and griddle for 2 minutes on each side until well charred and fully cooked through. Try to turn only once to make sure you get neat lines: partially lift up a slice to see how the gridding is going and if the satisfying char lines are there, turn them; if not, lay the slice back down and continue to cook.

3. Toast the walnuts on a tray in the oven for 10 minutes.

4. Remove the aubergine from the griddle and transfer to a plate: stack the slices on top of each other in towers. The residual heat encourages them to cook.

5. Mix the yoghurt and garlic together with a good pinch of crushed salt flakes.

6. Meanwhile, place the butter in a small saucepan and melt over a medium heat. Watch it carefully as you don't want it to burn. Allow the butter to bubble and the solids to begin to gently brown. Once the butter begins to go a rich golden colour, remove from the heat. The butter will keep cooking in the residual heat of the pan. Place a small bowl to the side and if it starts to go too far, decant it into the bowl to stop the cooking. You can always stop and then cook a little further, so don't rush. Once done, stir in a pinch of salt.

7. Spoon the yoghurt mixture onto a platter or plate individually, if you like. Lay over the aubergine slices. Top with the branches of tomatoes and any individual tomatoes that have fallen loose. Break up the walnut into large pieces and add. Finally liberally spoon the brown butter over everything.

Roast *aubergine* with cannellini bean stew

This is great cooked on a barbecue, where the vegetables take on a lovely smokiness. Or this recipe can be adapted to transform leftover vegetables from yesterday's barbecue. Space depending, it also works extremely well inside on a griddle, so all is well if the weather turns. This dish is reminiscent of a caponata but a bit lighter.

SERVES 4

- 2 yellow peppers (red are also fine)
- 3 aubergines
- 2 courgettes
- 2 tablespoons olive oil
- 2 celery sticks, cut into roughly 2cm (¾ inch) lengths
- 100g (3½oz) cherry tomatoes, halved across the equator
- 2 tablespoons capers, drained (rinse if salted)
- 240g (8½oz) cooked cannellini beans (120g/4¼oz dry weight)
- 1 tablespoon sherry vinegar or red wine, or to taste
- sea salt flakes
- 2 tablespoons extra-virgin olive oil, to serve

1. Preheat the oven to 200°C (400°F), Gas Mark 6.

2. Place the peppers on a tray and roast in the oven for 40 minutes until collapsed and the skin is lifting from the flesh. Remove and place in a bowl with a plate snuggly fitted on top. Allow them to steam and cool down as the skins release.

3. Heat a griddle pan over a medium-high heat and place the aubergines and courgettes on whole. Cook for 20–30 minutes, turning them a quarter of a time every now and then until slightly charred on the outside and cooked through. They will be done at different times, so when each is ready pull them off and reserve until all the others are done. Peel the aubergines of their blackened skins, then slice the aubergines and courgettes down the centre and into large chunks.

4. Peel the peppers: by now the skins will easily slip off the flesh like jackets. Also remove the stalks and seeds, but don't drive yourself mad getting every seed: a few aren't an issue. Tear the peppers into strips.

5. Add the oil to a pan big enough to hold everything over a medium heat. Follow with the celery and cook gently for 5 minutes until beginning to soften. Add the tomatoes along with 125ml (4fl oz) water, and cook for 3 minutes.

6. Add the capers and beans and warm through for 2 minutes. Add the remaining vegetables and stir gently to combine everything. Remove from the heat and add salt and vinegar to taste. Spoon into bowls and dress with the extra-virgin olive oil.

Aubergine parmigiana

This is indulgent but not overly rich. Grilling the aubergines adds a touch of smokiness and dramatically reduces the amount of oil involved. I often used to have a plate of parmigiana from a local Italian café on my lunch break when I lived in Leeds. The café was one of those old-school places where the grandmother is still running the show. As was the case then with the prepared dishes, this is great eaten the next day or beyond that, when the flavours have really married together. Additionally you can happily assemble the day before and keep in the refrigerator overnight before baking. Let the parmigiana set for about 30 minutes once out of the oven, as this helps everything stay together and lessens the molten lava effect. I like to serve with a simple green salad or sliced cucumber lightly dressed in vinegar.

SERVES 4–6

FOR THE SAUCE
- 2 tablespoons olive oil
- 1 red onion, roughly diced
- 8 garlic cloves, sliced
- 100ml (3½fl oz) white wine
- 2 × 400g (14oz) cans plum tomatoes
- 1 tablespoon dried oregano
- 3 tablespoons extra-virgin olive oil

FOR THE PARMIGIANA
- 1–2 tablespoons olive oil
- 4 aubergines, sliced lengthways about 1.5–2cm (5/8–¾ inch) thick
- 100g (3½oz) Parmesan or hard cow's cheese, finely grated or blitzed in a spice grinder or food processor
- 125g (4½oz) breadcrumbs
- 20g (¾oz) basil, leaves picked
- 500g (1lb 2oz) mozzarella, drained and sliced
- sea salt flakes and black pepper

1. Heat the oil in a medium pan over a medium heat. Add the onion and cook for about 10 minutes until starting to turn translucent. Add the garlic and cook for 1 minute. Add the wine and let the alcohol bubble off for 30 seconds.

2. Add the tomatoes and oregano, then half-fill each tomato can with water and add, rinsing out the cans as you go. Roughly break or split open the tomatoes with a spoon. Gently simmer for about 20–30 minutes until reduced and thickened.

3. Remove from the heat and allow to cool slightly. Blend with the extra-virgin olive oil until mostly smooth. Season with salt and pepper.

4. Heat a griddle pan over a medium heat. Coat the aubergines with a tablespoon of olive oil and, working in batches, grill on each side for 4–6 minutes until lightly charred and cooked through. When done, I stack them on top of each other for residual cooking.

5. Preheat the oven to 200°C (400°F), Gas Mark 6. Spoon some sauce on the base of a 25 × 15cm (10 × 6 inch) baking dish, followed by a scattering of Parmesan and a small handful of the breadcrumbs and basil leaves. Top with a layer of aubergine, cutting them to fit if needed. Repeat the layering in this manner but adding some of the mozzarella after the sauce each time. Finish with a layer of sauce, cheese and breadcrumbs.

6. Drizzle with the remaining oil and bake in the oven for 40–50 minutes until golden and bubbling.

7. Remove from the oven and allow to stand for 20–30 minutes before serving.

Roasted or raw, **PEPPERS** add such a wonderful vibrancy to dishes. If you have the time and are roasting them from fresh, it is worth going slow and diligently, making sure they cook evenly. There is nothing quite like the juicy flesh of a perfectly roasted pepper. They keep so well in the refrigerator as well. It is definitely worth having a stash to go into salads and sandwiches.

Flame-roasted *jalapeños* stuffed with ricotta

These are a delicious canapé or start to a meal. The twang of green pepper and spiciness are balanced perfectly with the cooling ricotta. You want them to be cooked but not completely giving, as they need to be sturdy enough to be picked up by hand. Fresh, plump, firm jalapeños are what– you need, so they can withstand the fire treatment. You can also cook these on a griddle pan in the kitchen if a barbecue isn't available.

SERVES 10 AS A CANAPÉ OR 4 AS A STARTER

- 20 jalapeño peppers
- 250g (9oz) best-quality ricotta
- 4 spring onions, 2 finely diced, 2 finely sliced
- 10g (¼oz) fresh coriander, handful of leaves picked, remaining leaves and stalks finely chopped
- 1 tablespoon extra-virgin olive oil, plus extra for drizzling
- sea salt flakes

1. Light a charcoal barbecue. When the flames have died down and the embers are glowing, you can begin. If using a griddle pan, get it smoking hot.

2. Using a pair of tongs, gently grill the jalapeños for 5-8 minutes until they get some colour on them, keep turning them throughout cooking. When the skins are charred and the flesh is soft, add them to a mixing bowl and cover.

3. Allow them to cool until they are able to be handled. Peel off as much of the skins as you can then slice the whole peppers in half, using the stalk so they all look even. Carefully remove the seeds and membrane with a spoon, or leave some of this intact if you desire a spicier result: eat one and gauge the level you prefer.

4. Mix the ricotta with the diced spring onion, chopped coriander leaves and stalks, reserving some for later use as toppings. Season to taste.

5. Stuff each evenly with a heaped teaspoon of ricotta mix. Arrange on a platter and drizzle with the oil making sure to get a decent amount onto each pepper so you have a little slick of it when eating each one. Scatter with the reserved sliced spring onions, coriander leaves and some salt and serve.

Romesco sauce

I have tried to make this store-cupboard friendly, so you can quickly knock this sauce up if you keep the ingredients in stock. I tend to always have these on hand. If you have more time and fancy roasting fresh red peppers, go for it. Throw them in the oven on a high heat until collapsing, then peel and deseed. This is good on anything and everything. I make it first and then dream up things to eat it with. It's great with anything grilled, used as a dressing for green beans, salad or even with onions that have been roasted whole as in the recipe on page 100 (also see opposite).

MAKES ABOUT 400ML (14FL OZ)

- – 100g (3½oz) almonds
- – 2 garlic cloves, unpeeled
- – 250g (9oz) good-quality roasted red peppers
- – 100g (3½oz) almonds
- – 2 garlic cloves, peeled
- – 50ml (2fl oz) extra-virgin olive oil
- – 3 tablespoons lemon juice
- – ½ bunch of parsley (about 15g/½oz), soft stalks as well as leaves
- – 1 teaspoon sweet paprika
- – 1 teaspoon hot smoked paprika
- – sea salt flakes and black pepper

1. Preheat the oven to 200°C (400°F), Gas Mark 6.

2. Place the almonds and garlic on a tray and roast in the oven for 7 minutes or so, until beginning to turn golden.

3. Place all the remaining ingredients in a blender or food processor. Pulse until well combined. I like the sauce with some texture. Check the seasoning and adjust accordingly. The sauce will keep well, covered, in the refrigerator for at least a week.

Roasted *red peppers* with spicy green sauce

I made the sauce first and worked backwards to create this recipe. The roasted peppers work amazingly; the plump, sweet flesh with the green sauce makes for a lovely dish. However do feel free to just make the sauce and use it freely wherever you like. Adding plain cooked grains like spelt or barley to the dish is a great way to make it more substantial. The sauce can be made ahead and kept in the refrigerator for three days, but after this it starts to lose its brightness. I like to make extra so I have some left over. Eat the sauce with eggs or use as a salad dressing; have alongside anything you want, to add herby freshness.

SERVES 4 AS A STARTER

- 6 red peppers
- 3 tablespoons extra-virgin olive oil
- 2 tablespoons sherry vinegar

FOR THE SPICY GREEN SAUCE
- 1–3 green chillies, whole or deseeded
- 100g (3½oz) fresh coriander, a few reserved for garnishing
- 100g (3½oz) mint, leaves picked, a few reserved for garnishing
- 150g (5½oz) yoghurt
- 3 tablespoons lemon juice, or more to taste
- sea salt flakes

1. Preheat the oven to 220°C (425°F), Gas Mark 7.

2. Place the peppers on a baking tray and roast for about 25 minutes, turning every 5–10 minutes or so until the flesh is collapsing and cooked through.

3. Meanwhile combine the sauce ingredients in a blender and blend until smooth, reserving some of the mint and fresh coriander for garnishing. Check the seasoning and adjust with salt and more lemon juice if desired. Set aside until needed.

4. Once the peppers are soft and collapsed, remove from the oven and then place them in a mixing bowl and cover tightly. Allow them to cool; they will steam and the skins will loosen from their flesh. Don't peek; just allow them to do their thing.

5. Once they are cooled, peel the skins, split the peppers and scrape out the seeds. Tear the peppers into thick strips, roughly 8–10 pieces per pepper. If they fall apart into more, you can leave them as halves. Combine the strips with the oil, vinegar and a pinch of salt. Mix to season them evenly.

6. Spoon out some sauce onto individual plates or a sharing platter. Place the dressed peppers, mint and coriander on top. Eat with crusty bread or as part of a larger meal.

BBQ *chilli* salsa

I love making this as a side project along with whatever else I'm cooking on the barbecue. It makes good use of the coals and a little goes a long way. I first made this on holiday when we were mainly cooking over fire and it became the condiment that went with everything. Feel free to play with the ratios and use what you have on hand, such as other colours of pepper. The recipe below will make just over a litre (1¾ pints) of salsa. I keep it a fairly thick salsa to spread rather than a sauce to pour. If you would like a thinner sauce, blend it really well and add a splash of water. The salsa keeps well for a few weeks in the refrigerator. Give it a stir to bring together before using.

MAKES 1 LITRE (1¾ PINTS)

- 3 onions, unpeeled
- 5 red peppers
- 5 long red chillies
- 5 tomatoes
- 5 garlic cloves, unpeeled
- 3 tablespoons extra-virgin olive oil
- 2 tablespoons cider vinegar, sherry or white wine vinegar, or more to taste
- honey or unrefined sugar (optional)
- sea salt flakes

1. Place the onions, peppers and chillies on a barbecue, plancha or grill or in a griddle pan over a medium-high heat. You want the skins to blister and blacken and the flesh to soften and cook through.

2. The chillies are quick: remove after 5 minutes, or when they are puffed and the skins start releasing from the flesh. Set aside to cool in a mixing bowl with a plate on top to help the skins further separate.

3. Keep turning the peppers to cook evenly. Once they are collapsing and blistered, after about 20 minutes, place in the mixing bowl and cover.

4. The tomatoes and garlic can be slightly tricky if using a barbecue grill with gaps, so place them in a small oven pan to contain them. Cook for 15–20 minutes until they collapse and soften. Again you want the skins to blister and release from the flesh, so get them as soft as you can; they take on the smoke flavour beautifully. Add them into the bowl and allow to cool slightly. The onions will take the longest, usually around 40–50 minutes. They want to be blackened outside and soft and collapsing inside.

5. When cool enough, peel the chillies, tomatoes and garlic and peel and deseed the peppers.

6. Pour the oil into a blender with the peeled chillies, peppers, tomatoes and garlic. Squeeze the tender insides of the onions into the blender. Add a good pinch of salt and the vinegar. Blend until smooth, taste and add more vinegar and salt, and the honey or sugar if needed, accordingly.

7. You should end up with just over 1 litre (1¾ pints). It will keep well, covered, in the refrigerator for a few weeks. It will marry and evolve once made, and you can always stir in another element at a later date if you feel its lacking once it's settled in the refrigerator for a while. Use on everything.

ASPARAGUS COURGETTES & GREEN BEANS

I adore **ASPARAGUS**. During its season I often just have a plate of simply steamed asparagus to myself for dinner. The best way to eat it is with melted butter, a judicious crack of black pepper and a light spritz of lemon – or maybe some aioli to dip the steamed tips into. But there comes a point, usually midway through the season, when I've eaten so much already that I look for some further expressions. By this time I've had so much I'm well on the way to looking like an asparagus.

Grilled *asparagus* & lemon rice

I like to cook this on a barbecue with the pan resting on a griddle plate as it takes on a subtle smokiness from the fire – but a griddle pan on the stove is as good. Great with leftover rice, as the freshness of the lemon brightens everything and gives it new life.

SERVES 4

- 3 tablespoons neutral oil (such as groundnut or sunflower)
- 1 onion, finely diced
- 1 celery stick, finely diced
- 1 leek, trimmed, cleaned and finely diced
- 3 garlic cloves, sliced
- 2 bunches of asparagus (500g/1lb 2oz), cleaned and woody ends snapped off
- 250g (9oz) cooked short grain brown rice (125g/4½oz dry weight)
- zest and juice of 1 lemon
- 100g (3½oz) hard sheep's cheese, such as pecorino, grated (optional)
- sea salt flakes and black pepper

1. Heat 2 tablespoons of the oil in a pan large enough to fit everything over medium heat. Add the onion, celery and leek with a good pinch of salt. Gently cook for 12 minutes to soften everything. Add the garlic and cook for a further 5 minutes.

2. Meanwhile, toss the asparagus in the final tablespoon of oil and a pinch of salt. Heat a griddle pan over medium-high heat and grill for about 5 minutes, turning once, until tender. Pull off a spear when you think they are approaching being done, slice a section off and eat it. If they need longer, return the spear and try again in a minute or so. Remove from the heat and slice each spear into roughly four or five sections.

3. Add the rice to the onion pan along with 100ml (3½fl oz) water to help everything get moving. Stir well but gently to reheat the rice but avoid breaking the grains. Add the asparagus and the lemon juice with a few good grinds of pepper. Stir to combine.

4. Spoon onto plates, or place the pan on the table for people to help themselves. Add the lemon zest and the cheese, if using.

Warmed *asparagus* & lettuce

This is a lovely way to take these fresh ingredients to the next level. Just taking the rawness away takes them to a different place. I love the mushrooms' welcome depth and earthiness, and this is why I like to keep mushroom stock cubes on hand as a way of quickly adding that flavour to dishes without soaking and chopping dried mushrooms. If you have the time and dried mushrooms to hand, do go down that route. If you do, adding the finely diced dried mushrooms is a welcome touch. Make sure to have lots of crusty bread to mop up the juices.

SERVES 4 AS A LIGHT STARTER OR SIDE

- 3 tablespoons olive oil
- 2 small onions, cut into eighths and separated into petals
- 500g (1lb 2oz) asparagus, woody ends snapped off, sliced 1cm (½ inch) thick on the diagonal
- 1 mushroom stock cube, dissolved in 200ml (7fl oz) hot water or mushroom soaking water (from 10g/¼oz dried mushrooms) or vegetable stock
- 4 heads of baby gem lettuce, quartered lengthways
- 15g (½oz) mint, leaves picked, finely chopped
- sea salt flakes and black pepper

1. Heat the oil in a large, deep frying pan over medium heat. Add the onions and cook for 10–12 minutes, stirring often, until the onions soften. They should still hold their integrity in the final dish, so don't cook them until collapsing.

2. Add the sliced asparagus to the pan and toss well to combine. Keep stirring for 1 minute, then add the stock. Simmer for 3 minutes.

3. Once the asparagus is tender, remove from the heat and add the lettuce, turn to coat with the cooking liquid and wilt the lettuce. Season to taste. Finally stir in the mint and serve.

Asparagus fritters & aioli

These are great as a pre-dinner snack or starter. The asparagus spears just cook through until tender with a crispy batter coating. It doesn't get much better than that. They are best eaten hot, dipped liberally in aioli. If you are using them as a canapé, send them out in batches as they are done, to be consumed while you are frying the rest. Go heavy on the lemon juice in the aioli as it works so well. I give two ways of making aioli: using the traditional whisking method and, if you would like an extremely quick method, using a hand blender. The blender method works best if you double the quantities. You don't add the garlic before blending, as garlic goes stale overnight in aioli; just stir it into the sauce when you want to use it.

SERVES 4 AS A STARTER OR 12 AS A CANAPÉ

FOR THE AIOLI
- 2 egg yolks
- 20g (¾oz) Dijon mustard
- 15g (½oz) white wine vinegar
- 2 garlic cloves, finely grated
- 175ml (6fl oz) neutral oil (such as groundnut or sunflower)
- 75ml (2½fl oz) extra-virgin olive oil
- squeeze of lemon juice, or to taste
- sea salt flakes

FOR THE ASPARAGUS FRITTERS
- 150g (5½oz) plain flour
- 300ml (10fl oz) sparkling water
- 500ml (17fl oz) sunflower oil, for frying (after using, sieve when cool and rebottle for another use)
- 24 spears asparagus, woody ends snapped off
- white wine vinegar (optional)
- sea salt flakes, finely ground

1. If taking the whisking route for the aioli, combine the egg yolks, mustard, vinegar and garlic in a bowl. Whisk together while adding the oils a drop at a time to begin with, then gradually increase the amount of oil as the emulsion begins to form. Keep going until you have used all the oil. Stir in a pinch of salt and a squeeze of lemon juice.

2. If using the quick method, you need a tall jug or container that fits all the ingredients and that just accommodates the hand blender: the narrower the better. Add all the aioli ingredients except the garlic. Place the hand blender in the jug right at the bottom. Blend on high holding the container in one hand and slowly bringing the blender away from the bottom. As you do so, the yolks will emulsify and you'll see the mixture go white and thick like mayonnaise. Go slowly to allow the yolks to properly form an emulsion. (If the mixture doesn't work, use the whisking method with a fresh egg yolk and trickle in the unemulsified mix.) Blitz in the garlic.

3. In a bowl, mix the flour and sparkling water together with a good pinch of salt until smooth.

4. Heat 5cm (2 inches) of oil in a deep, 24cm (10 inch) frying pan to 190°C (375°F), or until a small cube of bread turns golden in 2 minutes.

5. Working in batches that fit in the pan, drop a few spears at a time into the batter. Turn them over in the batter and swiftly lay them side by side in the pan. Fry for 2–3 minutes until the underside is golden, then turn them to fully cook the second side for 1–2 minutes. They are done when the batter is golden.

6. Drain on kitchen paper. Serve straight away, stacked up, sprinkled with the vinegar, if using, with the lemony aioli alongside.

A cornerstone of summer and late summer eating. Wonderful finely sliced and eaten raw, grilled or roasted, **COURGETTE** is an all-round champion performer. If you find yourself with larger specimens, slice them into quarters along their lengths and then cut out the soft centre and seeds. In larger courgettes this tends to be just filled with water and doesn't add anything to the end dish. It's better to remove this and leave behind the firmer flesh. I love eating younger courgettes raw, sliced in salads or stirred into soups at the last minute for some crunch.

Courgette, butter bean, onion & basil salad

Salads of this nature are a mainstay of my lunch: light but with enough flavour and substance to carry me through the afternoon. Let the ingredients evolve as the seasons change and based on what you have on hand. Don't be afraid to swap in other bits of fresh crunchy veg or herbs. This is perfect enjoyed outside in the sun with a glass of white wine to help ease yourself into the afternoon.

SERVES 2 AS A SIDE OR 1 AS LUNCH

– 1 Tropea onion, or 3 spring onions, sliced very finely into rounds
– good-quality red wine vinegar, to taste
– 2 small courgettes, finely sliced by hand or on a mandolin
– 1 tablespoon capers
– 20g (¾oz) basil, roughly chopped
– 3–4 tablespoons extra-virgin olive oil, or to taste
– 325g (11½oz) cooked butter beans
– sea salt flakes
– a healthy pinch of chilli flakes, to serve

1. Separate the onion rings in a large mixing bowl. Add a decent slug of the red wine vinegar to take the edge off the onions and slightly temper them.

2. Add the sliced courgettes to the bowl. Add the capers and basil to the bowl, along with the oil and butter beans.

3. Toss to combine, add some salt, check the seasoning and add more salt, vinegar and oil if needed. You are looking for a punchy, well-seasoned mixture brought together with a good slick of oil. Arrange in a bowl or serving platter and scatter liberally with chilli flakes to serve.

Whole *courgettes*
with caramelized onions

Many of my recipes are created from what is available in the market; they evolve over time and are by no means set in stone. This one in particular came about due to the sublime organic produce we acquired on holiday at a French market. Simply cooked, the ingredients amount to more than the sum of their parts. I added the chilli when I cooked it for a friend from Pakistan. You could also stir through some basil at the last minute, or some dill or mint. Herbs are always welcome! It's best to slice the onions Lyonnaise, which is to cut across the onion from root to top, rather than across the grain; this results in the onions keeping their shape when cooked, rather than breaking down. But as always, swap elements in and out according to what is available and your personal taste.

SERVES 4 AS PART OF A MEAL

- 3 onions, sliced Lyonnaise
- 4 tablespoons good-quality olive oil
- 8 young, firm, small–medium courgettes (baby courgettes are excellent here – just watch the cooking time)
- 3 garlic cloves, sliced
- a healthy pinch of chilli flakes (optional)
- sea salt flakes

1. In a frying pan, fry the onions in the oil with a healthy pinch of salt over a medium-low heat for 10–12 minutes until starting to brown.

2. Meanwhile, trim the ends of the courgettes and the woody part of the stems, leaving some intact; they are perfectly edible.

3. Reduce the heat to medium–low. Add in the garlic and chilli flakes, if using, then place in the courgettes, turning them to coat them as best you can with the onions and garlic. Gently cook them whole for 20–30 minutes, turning them occasionally, until a knife point can be easily pushed all the way through and the onions have caramelized. If the onions begin to brown too much or the mixture seems too dry, add a splash of water or even put a lid on to help steam the courgettes a bit.

4. Remove from the heat and allow to cool for a few moments. Serve at the table in the pan or on a platter.

Courgette & herb lasagne

I'm not one to stray too far from the acid twang of a tomato sauce, but this is a real winner for a summertime lasagne fix. The greens provide freshness but also an earthiness that keeps everything in check. This is great with a salad of bitter leaves in a simple olive oil and lemon juice dressing. Making the pasta in a mixer really takes the work out of it. Once you've done it a couple of times it will feel like second nature. Use 500g (18oz) of fresh pasta sheets if you are in a hurry.

SERVES 6 GENEROUSLY

FOR THE PASTA
– 400g (14oz) 00 flour, plus extra
  for dusting
– 4–5 eggs
– 4 tablespoons extra-virgin olive oil
– salt

FOR THE BÉCHAMEL SAUCE
– 75g (2¾oz) butter
– 75g (2¾oz) plain flour
– 1 litre (1 ¾ pints) milk
– ½ a nutmeg

FOR THE LASAGNE
– 1kg (2lb 4oz) courgettes (about 6)
– 8 tablespoons extra-virgin olive oil
– 2 small onions, finely sliced
– 400g (14oz) spinach
– 25g (1oz) parsley
– 250g (9oz) ricotta
– 150g (5½oz) Parmesan, grated
  or blitzed in a food processor to
  breadcrumb consistency
– 50g (1¾oz) basil, tough stalks
  removed
– 3 tablespoons lemon juice
– sea salt flakes and black pepper

1. Combine the flour, 4 of the eggs, the olive oil and a good pinch of salt in a stand mixer with a dough hook. Start kneading on a medium–low speed. Once the ingredients are on their way to forming a dough, increase the speed to medium. Knead for about 5 minutes. If it is a little dry and looking like breadcrumbs, add either a splash of water or an egg. Equally if it's too wet, add a tablespoon of flour at a time until the dough has a firm consistency.

2. Transfer the dough to a chopping board and then invert the bowl over it. Let it rest for 30 minutes. Preheat the oven to 200°C (400°F), Gas Mark 6.

3. Slice the courgettes into 5mm (¼ inch) thick rounds with a mandolin, otherwise slice as finely as you can with a knife. Toss with a pinch of salt and 4 tablespoons of the oil, then lay them evenly spaced on a baking tray or two. Roast the courgettes for about 20–30 minutes, turning once with a spatula, until beginning to turn golden. Remove from the oven and set aside. Reduce the oven to 180°C (350°F), Gas Mark 4.

4. To make the béchamel, melt the butter together with the flour in a medium saucepan over medium heat and cook gently, stirring constantly for 5 minutes. The flour should begin to toast a little and become slightly golden with a nutty aroma; it's all flavour and cooks the flour out, so don't worry as long as it doesn't go too dark. Add the milk, 100ml (3 ½fl oz) at a time, and stir vigorously to incorporate. Repeat until the milk is added and the sauce is smooth. Grate in the nutmeg and add a pinch of salt. Cook for about 5–10 minutes until the sauce loosely coats the back of a spoon. Set aside.

5. Heat 2 tablespoons of the olive oil in a large frying pan over medium heat, add the onions and cook gently for 10-15 minutes until very soft. Then add the spinach and parsley, cook for a few minutes until well wilted. Set aside spread on a plate to cool a little.

6. In a food processor, add the cooled spinach and parsley mixture along with a good pinch of salt, black pepper to taste, the ricotta, 100g (3 ½oz) of the Parmesan, basil, lemon juice and 2 tablespoons of olive oil. Process until smooth.

7. Divide the pasta dough into quarters and run through a pasta machine until the penultimate width setting. Dust with flour and set aside while repeating with the remaining dough. Cut the pasta into rough lengths that will fit your oven dish. Keep the smartest ones for the top.

8. In a 35 × 25cm (14 × 10 inch) oven dish, spoon enough béchamel to cover the base. Then add a handful of the courgettes and a couple more spoonfuls of béchamel. Follow with a sheet of pasta. Then add a quarter of the remaining courgettes, a quarter of the remaining green spinach sauce and a couple of spoonfuls of béchamel. Repeat this three more times, making sure to hold back about a third of the total béchamel for the top. Finish with a layer of pasta, then spread the remaining béchamel over the top. Top with the remaining Parmesan.

9. Bake in the oven for 50 minutes, or until crispy on the edges and golden on top. Remove from the oven and let stand for 20 minutes or so before serving.

Caponata

Over the years I have cooked and made various versions of this dish. The one that resonates with me the most is made by keeping the vegetables in larger chunks, as opposed to the more 'saucy', finer-cut versions. Keeping the vegetables in larger pieces helps to allow the individual elements to have their own voice while still being a part of the gang. This is by no means a traditional version; it is merely the way I like it. I use slender aubergines, as the more slender and firm, the fewer seeds, and olives that haven't been pitted, but remember to warn guests about the pits! I often have it for lunch, topped with a spoonful of yoghurt and dressed with fresh herbs – basil, dill and coriander are good here. This is definitely not traditional, and taking on more of the role of an imam bayildi at this point, but hey ho!

SERVES 8

- 4 tablespoons extra-virgin olive oil, plus more to serve
- 2 onions, quartered
- 3 celery sticks, including leaves, cut into 4cm (1½ inch) lengths
- 1 head of garlic, cloves peeled and crushed roughly under heel of knife
- 50g (1¾oz) pine nuts
- 40g (1½oz) capers
- 50g (1¾oz) raisins
- 1 tablespoon honey
- 4 tablespoons red wine vinegar
- 8 tomatoes, skinned and chopped, or 2 × 400g/14oz cans whole plum tomatoes, cut into eighths
- 3 firm, slender aubergines, halved and sliced lengthways on the diagonal
- 4 courgettes, cut into 4cm (1½ inch) chunks, or 12 whole baby courgettes
- 180g (6oz) green olives (not pitted)
- sea salt flakes

1. Preheat the oven to 190°C (375°F), Gas Mark 5.

2. Heat the oil in a deep pan over a medium heat and add the onions and celery. Cook for 10 minutes until they have given way a bit and begun to colour. Add the garlic cloves then the pine nuts, capers and raisins. Stir for a few moments until the pine nuts have toasted slightly and then add the honey, followed by the vinegar. Then add the tomatoes and cook for 20 minutes.

3. Meanwhile, coat the aubergines in oil and a sprinkle of salt, then place on a baking tray and roast in the oven for 20–30 minutes, turning occasionally, until the pieces are golden brown but still holding their form. Set aside.

4. Once the tomatoes have begun to thicken slightly, add the courgettes and stir to immerse them in the sauce. Gently cook for a further 15–25 minutes, by which time the tomatoes will have formed a sauce and the courgettes will be giving way.

5. Add the aubergine. Stir to incorporate and simmer for a further 10 minutes until the vegetables are cooked, well coated in sauce, but still holding their form.

6. Once a sloppy but not loose stew-like consistency is formed, remove from the heat, stir in the olives and allow to rest. The longer the caponata sits, the greater the flavour. Check the seasoning and adjust if needed. Depending on your mood and the desired use of the caponata, serve it naked as a side, or on its own with a chunk of good bread and a drizzle of oil.

GREEN BEANS are one of the joys of the warmer months. Piled up on the table, they are so satisfying to eat presented in any manner. I love their vibrant green energy. Crunchy and fresh in salads or more sultry cooked with cream or braised, they are blissful either way. Do try and find the slimmest, younger beans, as they tend to be less tough and require less cooking.

Lemon butter
green beans

So simple, so quick and so good. This is great eaten as part of a meal or goes well as a side to pretty much anything. Add a fried or boiled egg to make it into more of a main dish. Some simply cooked fish would be wonderful with them.

SERVES 4 AS PART OF A LIGHT LUNCH OR A STARTER

- 125g (4½oz) unsalted butter
- sprig of thyme
- pinch of chilli flakes (optional)
- zest and juice of 1 lemon
- 450g (1lb) green beans, topped (leave the tails for presentation)
- sea salt flakes and black pepper

1. In a sauté or frying pan that will accommodate the beans, melt the butter with the thyme and chilli flakes, if using, over the lowest heat. (I like to place this pan on top of the pan of boiling water that I'm using for the beans, as the steam provides just the right amount of heat.)

2. Add the lemon zest and 1 tablespoon of the lemon juice, then stir or whisk to combine well. Add salt and pepper to taste, along with more lemon juice, if you like. Set aside while you cook the beans.

3. Bring a pan of well-salted water to a boil. Blanch the beans for 3–5 minutes until they still just retain some bite.

4. Drain the beans well and add them to the pan. Toss to coat completely with the lemon butter. Try a bean: add more lemon juice or seasoning if needed and serve straight away.

Bobby bean
vinaigrette with cheesy mash

This is one of those dishes where both parts together really set each other alight. It appears quite simple on the outset but the interplay with the vinaigrette and cheesy mash will keep drawing you back in. If you want to be slightly more virtuous and maybe less intense, say for lunch, the potatoes can be blitzed with 50g (1¾oz) butter instead. I like to leave the skins on for nutrients and flavour. I'm never keen to throw away parts that are perfectly good to eat. Just make sure they are well cleaned of soil. The mash can be made ahead and reheated in a pan when ready to serve; heat slowly and add a splash of milk to help it along.

SERVES 4

- 1kg (2lb 4oz) floury potatoes (such as King Edward or Maris Piper), cut into even chunks
- 1 small red onion, finely diced
- 2 tablespoons white wine vinegar
- 1 tablespoon Dijon mustard
- 2 tablespoons extra-virgin olive oil
- 400g (14oz) extra-fine green beans, topped (leave the tails for presentation)
- 240g (8½oz) Reblochon or other easy-melting cheese, such as Taleggio, cut into chunks
- 10g (¼oz) parsley, leaves picked and finely chopped
- sea salt flakes and black pepper

1. Bring a pan of salted water to a boil. Simmer the potatoes for 15–20 minutes until tender.

2. Meanwhile in a bowl, mix the onion with the vinegar, mustard and oil. Set aside and allow to sit until ready to serve.

3. Bring another pan of salted water to a boil. Blanch the bobby beans for 3–5 minutes until just tender. Drain the beans and place in the vinaigrette with the parsley.

4. Drain the potatoes. I like to add them with the cubed cheese to a food processor and blend until smooth. Be careful not to over blitz, just enough to incorporate the cheese. Otherwise mash the potatoes by hand and stir in the cubed cheese until incorporated.

5. Give the mash another good stir, then spoon onto plates. Follow with the dressed beans with any vinaigrette left behind in the bowl.

Green beans with
shallot & garlic cream
& toasted breadcrumbs

This sultry little number is a great start to a meal or works well as a lunch option. It reminds me of eating in bistros in Paris. I've played with it a little by adding breadcrumbs, and I feel the crunch is most welcome. It would work well with some black olives finely chopped and toasted with the breadcrumbs. The sauce and the breadcrumbs can be made ahead, so that when it comes time to serve you can just blanch the beans and toss them in the sauce to coat.

SERVES 3 AS A LIGHT LUNCH OR 4 AS A STARTER

- 125g (4½oz) old bread, blitzed to fine breadcrumbs
- 3 tablespoons olive oil
- 1 small onion or 3 shallots, finely diced
- 2 small garlic cloves, finely grated or crushed to a paste with salt
- 100ml (3½fl oz) crème fraîche
- 2 teaspoons Dijon mustard
- 400g (14oz) extra-fine green beans, topped (leave the tails for presentation)
- 10g (¼oz) parsley, leaves picked and finely sliced
- extra-virgin olive oil, for drizzling
- sea salt flakes and black pepper

1. Preheat the oven to 180°C (350°F), Gas Mark 4.

2. Toss the breadcrumbs in half the olive oil and spread evenly on a baking tray. Bake the breadcrumbs for 10–18 minutes until toasted and golden. Remove from the oven and set aside.

3. Heat the remaining olive oil in a pan over a medium heat, add the onion or shallots and a pinch of salt, then cook for 10 minutes. Add the garlic and cook for a further 3 minutes. Add the crème fraîche, then bubble away for 1–2 minutes until slightly reduced. Take off the heat and stir in the mustard. Check the seasoning and set aside.

4. Boil the green beans in salted boiling water for 3–5 minutes until just tender.

5. Drain and toss the beans with the onion mixture and the parsley. Arrange the dressed beans on plates and top with the toasted breadcrumbs. Drizzle with extra-virgin olive oil.

Bobby beans with smashed roasted tomatoes, red onion, capers & basil

A salad bursting with summer flavours. I can't get enough of this salad when green beans start appearing in the summer. If left alone I could easily sit down and finish off this whole serving. I love the balance of the tanginess from the tomatoes and vinegar with the crunchy onion and salty capers all draped over just-cooked green beans. Absolute heaven. This is best eaten, if possible, outside in the sun – with some wine and crusty bread.

SERVES 4

- 6 tomatoes, halved across the equator
- 4 tablespoons extra-virgin olive oil, plus extra to dress
- 1 red onion or 2 Tropea onions, finely sliced
- bunch of basil, leaves picked
- 30g (1oz) capers
- 500g (1lb 2oz) green beans, topped
- 3 tablespoons red wine vinegar
- sea salt flakes and black pepper

1. Preheat the oven to 160°C (325°F), Gas Mark 3.

2. Arrange the tomatoes cut-side up on a baking tray. Season with salt, pour over 2 tablespoons of the oil and roast for 1 hour. They should be juicy but the flavours concentrated. I normally do a bigger batch of these as they keep well in the refrigerator, and can be used in many different ways.

3. While the tomatoes are cooking, add the onion to a mixing bowl along with the basil leaves and capers.

4. Once the tomatoes are done, blanch the beans in salted boiling water for 3–5 minutes until tender. They should be cooked through but not overly floppy; test one when you feel they are almost done. I like to refresh them briefly in cold water to stop the cooking but keep them at room temperature rather than ice cold. Drain.

5. Add the beans to the mixing bowl with the remaining olive oil. Crush the tomatoes either with your hand, if cool enough, or with the back of a wooden spoon and add to the bowl. Season with vinegar to taste, start with a tablespoon and add to your taste. Stir everything around a few times to combine with a couple of coarse grinds of black pepper. Arrange on a serving plate. Drizzle with extra olive oil if you like.

Green bean fritters
with chilli mayo

Dredging clumps of crispy green beans through chilli sauce-spiked mayonnaise is rather a wonderful way to eat. This pairs well with a cold beer and friends. I like to pile the lightly coated green beans into the oil to encourage a bit of clumping, but do still cook in manageable batches, draining each before piling onto a plate. Then you can tear away sections when you eat for a perfect dredging apparatus. In terms of adding chilli to the mayonnaise, play with your favourite sauce options. Go with hot sauce for more of a vinegar-led kick or choose chilli rayu for a more spicy funk.

SERVES 4 AS A STARTER, SNACK OR CANAPÉ

- 3 egg whites
- 300g (10½oz) rice flour (plain flour is also fine)
- 500ml (17fl oz) sparkling water
- 500ml (17fl oz) neutral oil (such as groundnut or sunflower), for frying
- 450g (1lb) green beans, topped (leave the tails for presentation)

FOR THE CHILLI MAYO
- 300ml (10fl oz) good-quality mayonnaise (shop-bought or homemade – see page 166)
- 2 tablespoons chilli sauce, or to taste

1. In a large bowl, beat the egg whites until fluffy with soft peaks. Whisk in the flour and sparkling water.

2. Heat the oil in a wide, deep pan until about 180°C (350°F) or a little bit of the batter fries well on contact.

3. Meanwhile mix together the chilli mayo ingredients.

4. Dredge the beans through the batter, allowing any excess to fall off. Gently lay the batter-covered beans in the pan, crisscrossing the beans to form tangled masses. Fry in batches for 3 minutes, turning once to cook evenly. Drain on kitchen paper and repeat until all the beans are cooked.

5. Arrange on a platter with the chilli mayonnaise in a deep dipping bowl. Take great pleasure in dredging chunks of green beans through the mayonnaise. These are also good combined in soft rolls and eaten as sandwiches.

Tomato & garlic braised
green beans

These beans are brilliant as is, but can be used as a base and taken in different directions. Use as a sauce for pasta such as tagliatelle, or add a tablespoon or so of crushed Szechuan peppercorns with the garlic to go more of a Chinese route. Stirring in a couple of beaten eggs and letting them cook in the sauce right at the end is a lovely addition. Adding the leaves of herbs such as oregano or marjoram gives an extra dimension, but don't overlook parsley, mint or basil: stir through big handfuls of leaves at the last minute. Make sure to eat this with something to mop up all the juices. It may feel like there is a lot of oil but it adds a luscious roundness. Make sure to use good-quality oil as it is such a main component.

SERVES 4 AS PART OF A LIGHT LUNCH OR A STARTER

- 5 tablespoons good-quality olive oil
- 5 garlic cloves, finely sliced
- 1 onion, finely sliced
- 400g (14oz) can whole plum tomatoes, roughly crushed
- pinch of chilli flakes (optional)
- 100ml (3½fl oz) white wine
- 450g (1lb) green beans, topped (leave the tails for presentation)
- bunch of herbs to serve (optional)
- sea salt flakes

1. Heat the oil over a medium heat, in a lidded pan big enough to easily accommodate everything. Add the garlic and onion. After 1–2 minutes, before the garlic starts to colour too much, add the tomatoes with a good pinch of salt and the chilli flakes, if using.

2. Bring to a boil, then add the wine and cook off the alcohol for 30 seconds. Add 300ml (10fl oz) of water and bring back to a boil. Then add the green beans, pushing them down to submerge them as much as possible.

3. Cook for 7 minutes until the beans are cooked through but still retain some bite. Or cook them further if you want them to be softer.

4. Remove from the heat, add the herbs, if using, then toss to combine well. Serve warm straight away, or eat at room temperature when the flavours have further married and intensified.

TOMATOES SWEETCORN & MUSHROOMS

When the **TOMATO** season gets into full swing it is a wonderful time of year. Fresh sliced tomatoes on toast for breakfast. Tomato salad with every meal. Roasted, diced or simply eaten as snack... You can't really go wrong. Arguably the tomato improves just about anything. I can't get enough; every year I promise myself I will eat more the next, as I always mourn the ending of the season. It is crucial to use tomatoes at peak ripeness to really get the most from them. However if they are starting to go over, they can be cooked into a sauce or roughly chopped and thrown into soups and stews. If they are a little under-ripe, slowly roasting in the oven can give them some more life by concentrating the flavour.

Tel Aviv *tomato* & basil salad with loads of garlic & tahini sauce

I had this dish of garlicky tomatoes in Tel Aviv and it really stuck with me; the creamy tahini underneath, the metallic twang of basil and the punch of raw garlic. It stands up to most things and is great as a course by itself. Seemingly simple, it packs more than is first apparent; it is more than the sum of its parts. The beauty of crowning the dish with the garlic is that people can choose how much they want to eat. Although as you eat more and the flavours meld together, you may find you develop a taste for its wicked punch. such a main component.

SERVES 4 AS A SIDE SALAD

- 200g (7oz) tahini
- 3 tablespoons lemon juice
- 500g (1lb 2oz) ripe tomatoes (a mix of colours is fine), cut into rough chunks
- 25g (1oz) basil, leaves picked
- 4 tablespoons extra-virgin olive oil
- 8 garlic cloves, finely grated or minced
- sea salt flakes

1. In a mixing bowl, add the tahini, half the lemon juice and a pinch of salt. Using a whisk combine with 125ml (4fl oz) cold water until smooth. Check the lemon juice and salt levels and adjust accordingly.

2. In a bowl mix the tomatoes with the basil leaves, oil and a good pinch of salt.

3. Add a pinch of salt to the garlic and either using the flat side of a chef's knife on a chopping board or in a pestle and mortar, grind the garlic to a paste.

4. Spread the tahini on a platter. Add the tomatoes, followed by the generous amount of garlic. As you spoon out portions, the elements will mix together.

Tomato, herb
& halloumi salad

Red, yellow and even green tomatoes, if used judiciously, all work really well here: use whatever you have. I find yellow have a lovely sweet softness for this recipe, so they are worth using if you can find them, but any mixture is good. If you season the cut tomatoes and set them aside ahead of time, the juices will release and mix with the other ingredients to make a delicious dressing. Get the best halloumi you can; look for a spongier block, less like set rubber. Throw in whatever herbs you like in copious amounts. I love that this dish is a versatile, simple celebration of its ingredients. Serve quickly so the cheese is still tender.

SERVES 4 AS A SIDE SALAD

- 800g (1lb 12oz) tomatoes (a mix of
  sizes and colours is good)
- 3 tablespoons extra-virgin olive oil
- 2 tablespoons cider vinegar (sherry
  vinegar is also fine)
- 300g (10½oz) halloumi
- 50g (1¾oz) herbs, such as basil, dill,
  chervil or coriander
- sea salt flakes and black pepper

1. Cut the tomatoes into random chunks. (I like to cut a cheek off, halve, and then cut sections off the tomato at angles until it is equally divided.) Sprinkle with salt and pepper, then add the oil and vinegar. Give it a good mix around and leave to stand.

2. Unfold the crease in each block of halloumi to separate the block into two large, flat pieces. Heat a frying pan over a medium-low heat. Add the halloumi, flat-side down, and cook for 2 minutes. Lift a piece to see how it's getting on; if it is golden and well crisped, flip and cook for a further 2 minutes on the other side.

3. Once the halloumi is nice and golden on both sides and warmed through, remove from the pan and slice 2cm (¾ inch) thick.

4. Tear the herb leaves into the tomato mixture. Toss to combine and spoon onto individual plates or a platter. Lay the halloumi over the top, spooning any remaining tomato liquid over the top.

Gazpacho

One of my father's favourite dishes, a sentiment that I wholeheartedly agree with. It's such a wonderful summer dish, using the best of what's on offer. One of those meals that if you see it on the menu at a restaurant, or away on holiday, it must be ordered. It's a good way to check the capabilities of the kitchen as well: this dish is an exercise in balance. While rather forgiving, it can go off piste if some elements get a bit too bolshie, so it's the cook's job to keep everything in check while letting all the ingredients shine. I do like to make this as a next-day tonic, for example using up some leftover tomato and onion salad. I'll add the other ingredients to the leftovers and let it all marinade together, then blitz it up and balance with more vinegar and oil. In that vein, feel free to play with the amounts of any ingredients to suit your preferences, but do make sure to add a decent amount of salt, oil and vinegar to help the flavours sing.

SERVES 4 GENEROUSLY OR 6 AS A STARTER

- 1 cucumber, peeled, deseeded and chopped
- 1 red pepper, stemmed, deseeded and chopped
- 1 green pepper, stemmed, deseeded and chopped
- 1kg (2lb 4oz) tomatoes, roughly chopped
- 4 spring onions or ½ onion, chopped
- 2 garlic cloves, roughly chopped
- 100g (3½oz) stale white bread, cut into chunks
- 2 tablespoons sherry vinegar, or more to taste
- 5 tablespoons extra-virgin olive oil, plus extra for drizzling
- sea salt flakes and black pepper
- crusty bread, to serve

1. In a large mixing bowl, add all the ingredients, holding back half the oil and the seasoning. Give everything a good squeeze with your hands to help release the juices. Let it stand for 30 minutes, or longer if possible.

2. Add the mixture to a blender with 1 tablespoon salt and blend until very smooth. Taste and adjust the seasoning as needed, it may also need more vinegar. Blend in the remaining oil until the soup has the texture and richness of flavour that you like. Chill for 1–2 hours until very cold. It can be made a day ahead no problem. It will be better for it.

3. Serve with crusty bread and drizzled with more oil and a twist of black pepper.

Beans in sherried *tomato* sauce

I guess this is essentially a fresh, vibrant beans on toast. But the beans are livened up with some sherry and the toast is oven-baked crisp breads. I'm not reinventing the wheel, but definitely making use of an age-old combination. The crisp breads can be made ahead and stored in a sealed container. They go well with anything. Try breaking them to form croutons or use as scoops for dips. The beans take well to being topped with herbs or cheese, or simply eat just the beans, some bread and good-quality oil over the top.

SERVES 6

- 2 tablespoons neutral oil (such as groundnut or sunflower)
- 2 onions, roughly diced
- 3 carrots, roughly diced
- 5 garlic cloves, roughly chopped
- 2 × 400g (14oz) cans plum tomatoes or 8 fresh tomatoes, roughly diced
- 200g (7oz) dry white beans, soaked and cooked (cannellini, haricot and coco are good here), or 500g (1lb 2oz) canned
- 3 tablespoons best-quality sherry vinegar, or to taste
- extra-virgin olive oil, for drizzling
- sea salt flakes and black pepper

FOR THE CRISP BREADS
- 6 tablespoons olive oil
- 1 large baguette or slender loaf, finely sliced

1. Preheat the oven to 180°C (350°F), Gas Mark 4.

2. Drizzle some of the oil on several large, flat baking trays, or work in batches. Lay the bread slices, evenly spaced, in a single layer on the trays. Gently rub the slices with the rest of the oil and flip them over to lightly coat each side with oil (too much and they tend to be a bit greasy when cooked). Bake in the oven for 25 minutes until golden and crisp, turning halfway through. Some will inevitably cook faster and some slower. If working in batches, pull out the done ones and replace with freshly oiled slices, essentially having a production line on the go, while you are making the beans.

3. Meanwhile, heat the oil in a pan over a medium heat and sweat the onions, carrots and garlic with a pinch of salt for about 15 minutes until soft. Add the tomatoes, roughly breaking them up with a spatula. Half-fill each can with water and add to the pan. Cook for 25 minutes until reduced but not too dry, topping up water as needed.

4. Blend the contents of the pan in a blender until smooth, then return to the pan. Add the cooked beans and then gently cook together for a further 30 minutes or longer, adding water if needed: the consistency should be loose but still amalgamated. Season with salt and pepper, then add the sherry vinegar to taste: you want the sharp, sweet twang of the vinegar to be a solid backbone of the sauce.

5. Serve drizzled with extra-virgin olive oil, the crisp breads, cracked over the top. Spanish tortilla goes well with the beans. Also great with whole roasted portobello mushrooms on top.

Tomatoes
cooked in crème fraîche with mint on toast

Perfect as a light lunch or late breakfast, this is great really anytime. Rub the bread with garlic for an extra kick. Use any tomato you have on hand. Slice or segment larger tomatoes and add ahead of really small ones. A lovely thing happens when the juices of the tomatoes and the crème fraîche bubble together and join forces.

SERVES 4

- 2 tablespoons good-quality olive oil
- 2 garlic cloves, finely grated or minced
- 500g (1lb 2oz) tomatoes, cut through the equator
- 200g (7oz) crème fraîche
- 15g (½oz) mint, leaves picked and very finely sliced, some leaves reserved for serving
- sea salt flakes and black pepper
- good-quality bread, thickly cut and toasted, to serve

1. In a large frying or sauté pan, heat the oil over medium heat. Once nice and hot, add the garlic and cook for 30 seconds. Add the tomatoes cut-side down. Leave them alone to cook for 2–3 minutes until softened. Then flip over to the skin side.

2. Add the crème fraîche. Boil for 1–2 minutes to slightly reduce the liquid. Remove from the heat once the tomatoes are starting to collapse.

3. Add the sliced mint leaves to the tomatoes. Shuffle
the pan to combine everything and season with salt and pepper to taste.

4. Spoon the mixture over the toast, scatter over the mint leaves and eat with gusto.

Roasted *tomatoes* with egg mayonnaise

This makes rather a relaxed lunch. I love laying out the different components and everyone tucking in: really good bread, crisp, shredded lettuce, creamy egg mayonnaise and beautifully juicy but concentrated tomatoes. In recent times, I've gone for potato sourdough loaves from local bakeries for this. They are made with potato flour and sometimes pieces of potato mixed through the dough. It's a wonderful platform for everything.

SERVES 4

- 8 very ripe large tomatoes (on the vine, if possible), halved across the equator
- 3 tablespoons extra-virgin olive oil
- 8 eggs
- 10g (¼oz) chives, finely sliced
- 5g (⅛oz) tarragon, leaves picked and finely chopped
- sea salt flakes and black pepper
- shredded lettuce, to serve

FOR THE MAYONNAISE
- 2 egg yolks
- 20g (¾oz) Dijon mustard
- 2 tablespoons lemon juice, or more to taste
- 15g (½oz) white wine vinegar
- 175ml (6fl oz) neutral oil (such as groundnut or sunflower)
- 75ml (2½fl oz) olive oil (not too bitter or strong), or to taste

1. Preheat the oven to 160°C (325°F), Gas Mark 3. Place the tomatoes cut-side up and evenly spaced apart on a baking tray. Drizzle with the oil and sprinkle with salt. Roast in the oven for 40–60 minutes, or until slightly shrivelled and the flesh starts to look jammier. They may need longer depending on their water content and size. They will intensify the longer they are in, but be careful not to let them dry out or the skins will colour too far.

2. To make the mayonnaise, add the egg yolks, mustard, lemon juice and vinegar to a bowl. Whisk slowly, then once combined slowly begin adding the neutral oil in a trickle while continuing to whisk. Once the mixture begins to thicken, add the oil a little quicker, but beware not to go too fast: as long as it is emulsifying then all is good. Make sure to give it a few proper beats with the whisk to make sure the oil incorporates well before adding another slug. Once all the neutral oil has combined, continue with the olive oil. Once added, taste and add salt and more lemon juice to your taste.

3. In a medium-sized pan of cold water, gently add the eggs and slowly bring to a very gentle simmer. Simmer for 2 minutes. Remove from the heat and leave in the water for 4 minutes. Drain and return the eggs to the pan. Either drop them or bash them around in the pan to crack the shells a bit, then cover with cold water and allow the eggs to sit for a couple of minutes to help the shells release from the egg whites and make them easier to peel.

4. Peel the eggs, then either grate or roughly chop them, depending on the texture you desire. Stir in the mayonnaise to taste. Add the chives and tarragon, along with some pepper.

5. Serve piled on bread with some shredded lettuce. Top with the roasted tomatoes halves and any juices spooned over.

Tomato broth with thyme dumplings

This is my interpretation of a dish that a friend, Tim, who was a member of my uncle's band, made for us when we visited his house in Cumbria many years ago. The band were playing a gig in a churchyard and I was lucky enough to be spectating and eating very well. The dish has always stuck with me over the years as one of the most delicious things I have eaten. I mean, what more can you ask for than a fresh, vibrant, summery tomato broth grounded by herb-flecked dumplings. A wonderful thing.

SERVES 4

FOR THE BROTH
- 3 garlic cloves, roughly chopped
- 1 onion, roughly chopped into chunks
- 1 leek, trimmed, cleaned and roughly chopped from root to green tip
- 1 fennel bulb, roughly chopped
- 2 carrots, roughly chopped
- 2 celery sticks, roughly chopped
- 1kg (2lb 4oz) tomatoes (on the vine, if possible)

FOR THE DUMPLINGS
- 5 sprigs of thyme, leaves picked, stalks reserved for the broth
- 100g (3½oz) vegetable suet or unsalted butter, frozen and coarsely grated
- 225g (8oz) self-raising flour
- sea salt flakes and black pepper

1. In a large pan, put all the ingredients for the broth, except for the tomatoes, and the thyme stalks. Cover with 3 litres (5 ¼ pints) water and bring to a simmer. Bubble away for 30 minutes and remove from the heat. Allow to stand for as long as possible: at least 1 hour, but aim for 3 hours, or overnight is best.

2. Preheat the oven to 200°C (400°F), Gas Mark 6. Put the tomatoes and thyme stalks on a roasting tray and cook in the oven for 20–30 minutes until the tomatoes begin to collapse and the skins are coming away. Remove from the oven and allow to cool to a temperature you can handle them.

3. Either pass the tomatoes through a moulin, discarding the skin and seeds, or peel away the tomato skins and push the tomato flesh through a sieve in batches, discarding the seeds. Strain the broth and combine with the tomato pulp, then season with salt. This tomato broth can be made ahead; it will develop in flavour the longer it sits.

4. To finish the dish, fill a large saucepan with the broth and bring to a simmer. In a bowl, stir the suet, thyme leaves and flour together with a pinch of salt and good grind of pepper. Gently stir in 150ml (5fl oz) cold water until it forms a dough. Shape the dough by rolling walnut-sized pieces of it in your hands, forming the dumplings. Drop the dumplings into the saucepan of broth as you go.

5. Once all the dumplings are in, bring the broth to a simmer and gently bubble away with the dumplings for 7–12 minutes until they are cooked through, with a lid on the pan if possible.

6. Serve in individual bowls or take the pot to the table for people to help themselves, then add a good grind of black pepper.

The appearance of ears of corn at the market is slightly bittersweet, as it marks the coming to a close of the summer. Or I suppose gives you a bit of a kick to make the most of barbecuing and eating outside. **SWEETCORN** has such a welcome burst of sweet creaminess and pairs so well with so many things. Just like with peas, I find that frozen sweetcorn is the way to go if you can't get the fresh ears, and arguably whenever it isn't in season, as its sweetness rapidly declines once it is picked.

Sweetcorn salad
with spelt & tomatoes

I love these kinds of grain salads that are balanced with a pop of fresh veg and can be loaded with herbs and vinegar to bring everything to life. This salad is actually better if made ahead and left to sit, preferably at room temperature. It can be used as a side or a standalone dish, and you can also add other herbs if you like, or peas or green beans are welcome additions.

SERVES 4 AS PART OF A LIGHT LUNCH OR 3 AS A MAIN

- 120g (4¼oz) spelt or pearl barley
- 2 banana shallots or Tropea onions or 6 spring onions, finely sliced
- 250g (9oz) tomatoes, halved if small, cut into chunks if large
- 3 tablespoons extra-virgin olive oil
- 2 tablespoons moscatel vinegar (sherry or cider vinegars are fine)
- 150g (5½oz) frozen or canned sweetcorn, or 2 small ears
- 15g (½oz) dill, finely chopped
- sea salt flakes and black pepper

1. Bring a pan of salted water to a boil. Cook the spelt or pearl barley for 40–60 minutes, or until tender. Drain and rinse under cold water until cool. Drain again and set aside.

2. In a large mixing bowl add the shallots or onions, tomatoes, oil, vinegar and a good pinch of salt. Give everything a good stir and set aside.

3. Bring a pan of salted water to a boil. If using frozen sweetcorn, blanch for 2–3 minutes, drain and add to a bowl of cold water. If using canned sweetcorn, simply drain and refresh in a bowl of cold water. Drain again, then add to the grains. If using fresh ears, boil for 10–12 minutes then cut the kernels from each one.

4. Add the grains and sweetcorn to the tomato mixture with the dill. Stir well to combine, then taste and adjust the seasoning. Serve on a platter for people to help themselves or on individual plates.

Cheddar chilli
cornbread

We made this from a friend's recipe back when I worked at the Towpath café. Using fresh corn, along with the cheese and chilli flecked throughout, I thought it was such a lovely way to liven up cornbread. It's great when sweetcorn is in season but it also works well with frozen corn so, happily, it can be made whenever you like. The cornbread is delicious eaten warm as is, with salted butter or with more cheese. If I find myself with some left over I like to toast it and slather with salted butter. It goes wonderfully crisp on the edges when you toast it the next day.

SERVES 8

- 5 eggs
- 500ml (17fl oz) milk
- 325g (11½oz) polenta
- 60g (2¼oz) plain flour
- 10g (¼oz) baking powder
- 200g (7oz) mature Cheddar, grated
- 200g (7oz) frozen sweetcorn, defrosted,
  or kernels from 2 ears of corn
- 4 chillies (use a mix of red and green),
  finely diced, with or without the seeds
- 10g (¼oz) salt flakes

1. Preheat the oven to 200°C (400°F), Gas Mark 6. Grease and line a 26 x 18cm (10 x 7 inch) tin. It can be any shape you please but you need some depth in the finished cornbread, so try not to go too much larger than 24cm (9½ inch) square. A cast-iron skillet would also work well here.

2. In a bowl, beat the eggs and add the milk, mixing to combine. Then add the rest of the ingredients and stir well to make sure everything is evenly dispersed.

3. Pour the mixture into the tin and then bake in the oven for 35–40 minutes, or until a knife comes out relatively clean. It doesn't want to be squeaky clean as that means it has cooked too far and may dry out. The resting time out of the oven will finish it off. Turn the tin halfway through cooking to avoid any hot spots.

4. Leave to cool for at least 15 minutes. This bit is important as the cornbread is still cooking in the middle, so hands off! Once it has rested remove by either lifting it out with the greaseproof paper and slicing or cutting into chunks or cutting and serving directly from the tin or skillet at the table for ease.

BBQ *corn on the cob*
with spicy paprika & lime butter

This sweetcorn dish has such a wonderful burst of flavour. The corn can be chopped into smaller sections and then tossed in the butter for less daunting helpings at the table. I like to use a 50/50 blend of sweet and hot smoked paprika.

SERVES 6 AS A STARTER OR SIDE, OR CUT INTO SECTIONS TO SERVE MORE

- 6 ears of sweetcorn, husk on
- 125g (4½oz) unsalted butter
- 10g (¼oz) smoked paprika
- zest and juice of 2 limes, or to taste, plus extra zest to serve
- sea salt flakes

1. One hour before you are going to cook your sweetcorn, submerge them in cold water to soak the husks. This will help to delay the husks burning and to steam the kernels inside. If using a barbecue, light it now so it is at the embers stage when you start cooking. Flames are the husks' enemy: you want the sweetcorn kernels to steam as well as char slightly inside the husks, not the husks to burn off and the sweetcorn to dry out.

2. Gentle. Slow. No rush. These words should be running through your head when making the butter sauce. In a pan, add the butter and paprika, along with salt and the lime zest. Over the lowest heat (or the side of the barbecue), extremely slowly heat the mixture and melt the butter. Remove from the heat and let it relax for a while, then reintroduce to the heat. The residual or diffused heat in the pan is your friend here: you want a creamy emulsion rather than a split sauce where the solids have separated. It will coat the corn better and is really satisfying to eat. That being said, no stress if you forget the butter for a moment and it goes too far; it will get you more or less the same result.

3. Once the sauce is warmed through, add the lime juice to taste.

4. Grill the corn evenly on a barbecue or plancha or in a griddle pan or cast-iron skillet over medium heat, turning evenly for 15–20 minutes. The outside husks will go black. This is fine: they are protecting the corn inside and allowing it to steam. Carefully peel back one of the husks: to check if the kernels are done, using a small knife, cut a couple of kernels free to taste. If they aren't done, replace the husk and cook for a bit longer, then retry when you think they are done.

5. To serve, peel back the husks and twist them to fashion a makeshift handle. Liberally brush the corn with the butter sauce and grate over some zest with a sprinkle of salt, if you like.

Creamed *corn*, soft-boiled egg & garlic chilli crisp

This garlic chilli crisp can and should go on everything and anything. I built this recipe backwards from it. The sweet, creamy corn and potatoes act as a wonderful platform for the fiery, floral oil. The crisp can be used to dress noodles, fried eggs or steamed vegetables like broccoli or greens, or stirred into egg-fried rice or crunchy veg salads, to name a few. It's worth having on hand to bring simple ingredients together into more of a meal. It will keep well in the refrigerator, sealed in a jar, for four weeks or so, or give as a gift.

SERVES 4 AS A LIGHT MEAL WITH A SALAD OR AS A STARTER

- 350g (12oz) frozen sweetcorn, or kernels from 4 ears
- 50g (1¾oz) unsalted butter
- 1 onion, finely diced
- 1 large potato (about 300g/10½oz), such as King Edward, Maris Piper, Désirée or Estima, cut into roughly 1cm (½ inch) cubes
- 200ml (7fl oz) full fat milk
- 4 eggs
- sea salt flakes

FOR THE GARLIC CHILLI CRISP
- 250ml (8½fl oz) neutral oil
- 1 large or 2 medium onions, finely diced
- 1 head of garlic, cloves peeled and evenly sliced
- 3 tablespoons chilli flakes
- 2 tablespoons Szechuan peppercorns, crushed
- 5 star anise
- 1 tablespoons sea salt flakes
- 1 teaspoon honey

1. To make the garlic chilli crisp, add the oil, onion and garlic to a medium sized saucepan and simmer for 20–30 minutes until golden but not too dark. You want to slowly drive the moisture from the onion and garlic; if you cook it too quickly they will burn. Just before the end, when the mix has slowed its bubbling and the garlic is nice and golden, add the chilli flakes, Szechuan peppercorns and star anise. Give a good turn around and remove from the heat. Mix in the salt and honey. Set aside until ready to use.

2. Set aside 100g (3½oz) of sweetcorn. Pulse the remaining kernels in a food processor five or six times until broken but not puréed. A hand blender is also fine, or roughly chop them with a knife.

3. Add the butter to a medium saucepan over a medium heat. Follow with the onion when the butter begins to foam. Stir around the pan for 10–12 minutes until translucent. Add the potato and cook for a further 10 minutes, stirring so nothing sticks. If the mixture gets a little dry, add a splash of water to keep things moving. Add the pulsed corn and milk. Cook over a medium heat for 1 minute, then reduce to a low heat, stirring often, for about 3 minutes until the mixture slightly thickens. Add the reserved kernels and cook for a further 2 minutes. Remove from the heat and keep warm. Season with salt to your taste.

4. Place the eggs in a medium-sized saucepan filled with cold water and cover with the lid. Heat over a medium heat until gently simmering. Remove from the heat and leave to sit in the water for 2 minutes. Drain the eggs and return to the pan. Shake it to break the shells, then fill with cold water, empty and refill with cold water. Let sit for a while until the eggs are cool enough to handle. Remove the shells and halve each egg.

5. Add the corn to a plate and top with two egg halves. Spoon over as much garlic chilli crisp as you like.

Oh, for the love of **MUSHROOMS**. I like to cook them rapidly at high heat for colour and to develop their flavour, while helping to keep them moist internally. Mushrooms don't need to be played with much as their flavour and texture are incredible.

Andrew's garlic
mushrooms

My friend Andrew would often make this dish for us to eat together when I visited. The mushrooms were usually a mix depending on what we could get at the time of year. And the butter was double the amount I use below. This one is not for the faint-hearted, but in the winter months it certainly warms you up and sets steady foundations. It is especially good if you've been out in blustery winds on a bracing walk, or on skateboards down winding country roads as we were on these visits. A loaf of crusty bread is essential to dip and mop up the juices. This is dish great around a campfire, tearing off pieces of said bread. Other herbs are also most welcome to the party: tarragon is particularly good.

SERVES 4

- 250g (9oz) unsalted butter
- 1kg (2lb 4oz) chestnut mushrooms, or other varieties (a mix is good), trimmed
- 1 head of garlic, cloves peeled and roughly chopped
- bunch of parsley, leaves finely chopped
- sea salt flakes and black pepper
- 2 crusty baguettes, to serve

1. In a large, heavy-based pan, melt half the butter over a medium heat until beginning to foam. Add the mushrooms and give them a turn around to coat them in butter. Cook for 3 minutes until they are starting to gain some colour.

2. Follow with the garlic and stir well to combine. Cook for a further 7 minutes, stirring well so nothing sticks, until the mushrooms are golden.

3. Add the remaining butter. Once it has melted, add a good pinch of salt and the parsley. Cook the parsley for 1 minute to take the rawness away. Grind in a healthy amount of pepper and check the salt, adding more if needed.

4. Place the mushrooms in deep bowls; they should be swimming in golden, green-flecked butter. Serve with the bread alongside to tear off chunks and dip into the molten garlic butter: gloriously guilty eating. Cider also pairs well!

Roasted *mushrooms* with garlic, pickle & lemon yoghurt sauce

This is really simple to make and shows off the mushrooms in all their glory. They get wonderfully crisp and golden roasting in the oven. By all means pan-fry them, but the oven is a more no-nonsense option. This is a brilliant option for a veggie burger offering: the best in my opinion. Using mushrooms as the main component in place of a burger makes sense for me. The sauce is made for layering in a sandwich or burger. Just add salad leaves.

SERVES 4 AS A LIGHT LUNCH

- 1 small onion, finely diced
- 60g (2¼oz) cornichons, finely diced
- zest and juice of 1 lemon
- 600g (1lb 5oz) king oyster mushrooms or other good-sized mushrooms, trimmed and halved lengthways
- 4 tablespoons neutral oil (such as groundnut or sunflower)
- 200g (7oz) yoghurt
- 2 garlic cloves, minced, or 1 heaped teaspoon garlic granules
- sea salt flakes

TO SERVE
- 100g (3½oz) bitter leaves (such as mustard greens, rocket, watercress, radicchio, chicory)
- crusty baguette, warmed in the oven

1. In a bowl, mix the onion and cornichons with the lemon juice and a pinch of salt. Set aside.

2. Crush a pinch of salt until fine. Place the mushrooms in a mixing bowl and coat with the oil and crushed salt.

3. If roasting the mushrooms in the oven, heat to 200°C (400°F), Gas Mark 6. Lay out on a large tray and roast for 15–25 minutes until tender inside and crisp on the outside. Turn two-thirds of the way through.

Alternatively, heat a griddle or cast-iron pan big enough fit all the mushrooms over a medium–high heat. (If the pan is not big enough, cook the mushrooms in batches and keep warm in the oven.) Place the mushrooms in the pan, cut-side down and grill without moving for about 4 minutes. Lift one carefully to check. When they are golden and crisp at the edges, turn over and cook on the other side for a further 4 minutes until soft and relaxed inside.

4. Mix the yoghurt, lemon zest and garlic with the onion mixture.

5. Divide the mushrooms between individual plates. Add a dollop of yoghurt sauce and a handful of leaves dressed in a little oil. Equally I like to serve the mushrooms piled up on a plate with the sauce in a bowl and the salad in another bowl for guests to help themselves. Enjoy with chunks of crusty baguette warmed in the oven.

Pancakes stuffed with creamy *mushrooms*

This is a lovely dish for those still, cold days when the sun decides to shine. This filling can just as easily be used for a pie with a puff pastry top as it can the pancakes. Or spoon onto rice or mix through pasta. The pancakes should be served warm with a fresh, vibrant salad. There's enough batter for 9–10 pancakes in case the first one sticks!

MAKES 8 PANCAKES

FOR THE PANCAKES

- 4 eggs
- 200ml (7fl oz) milk
- 2 tablespoons vegetable oil, plus extra for frying
- 200g (7oz) plain flour
- pinch of salt
- knob of butter

FOR THE CREAMY MUSHROOMS

- 50g (1¾oz) butter
- 2 onions, finely diced
- 1 leek, trimmed, cleaned and finely diced
- 600g (1lb 5oz) mixed mushrooms (chestnut, button, oyster and chanterelles), trimmed and broken into thumb-sized chunks
- 150ml (5fl oz) white wine or cider
- 10g (¼oz) dried porcini mushrooms, soaked in 400ml (14fl oz) boiling water
- 15g (½oz) tarragon
- 150g (5½oz) crème fraîche
- salt and freshly ground black pepper

1. In a large Pyrex jug or mixing bowl with a spout, beat the eggs, then whisk in the milk and oil until combined. Stir in the flour and salt. Set aside to rest, covered, in the refrigerator for 30 minutes.

2. Add the butter to a wide-bottomed pan over a medium heat. Sweat the onion gently for 10 minutes, then add the leek, mixing well to coat with butter.

3. Cook the onion and leek for 2–3 minutes until they have relaxed, then add the fresh mushrooms. Increase the heat to high to help get them going: you want to get some colour and caramelization on the mushrooms before they start to give up their juices. Cook for 5 minutes in the pan, turning a few times but allowing them to rest on the bottom of the pan to enable colouration.

4. Add the wine or cider and allow the alcohol to bubble off for 30 seconds, then add the stock from the dried porcinis and finally the rehydrated mushrooms themselves after chopping through them roughly. Turn the heat back down to medium and let the mixture simmer away gently for 20–30 minutes. You want the liquid to evaporate, but don't allow the mix to catch.

5. Take the pan off the heat and stir in the tarragon, then the crème fraîche and some black pepper. Taste for seasoning and adjust accordingly. Set aside while you make the pancakes.

6. Retrieve the pancake batter from the refrigerator. Warm a suitable frying pan, 28cm (11 inch) ideally, over a medium–low heat. Add a splash of oil and brush it around the pan with kitchen paper, removing most but leaving a slick. Ladle or pour in enough batter to evenly cover the base of the pan, turning the pan as you do to aid this. Gently cook for 1–2 minutes until the pancake is firm enough to flip. (You don't need too much colour at this stage as they will be recooked.) Cook on the other side for 1 minute until set and then remove from the pan. Repeat for seven more pancakes.

7. Put an eighth of the mushroom mixture in the middle of each pancake, flattening it out slightly. Fold the top, bottom and side edges to form a parcel. Make sure the edges overlap a bit to help secure them.

8. Heat the frying pan over a medium heat, with a knob of butter and a splash of oil. Carefully place the mushroom parcels in (if you can fit more than one in the pan), fold-side down. Cook for 2–3 minutes until golden and then flip over. Cook for 2–3 minutes on the other side until it is a lovely, mottled golden brown, the filling is warm and the pancake crispy outside.

Mushroom
& chard stroganoff

This dish reminds me of my childhood. I used to travel around a lot dog-showing with my mother. It was a wonderful time, the weekends spent camping and barbecuing. Also the pit-stop pub visits on the long journeys home. As a vegetarian twenty odd years ago, I often found the pub mainstay was the mushroom stroganoff, if I was lucky, dusted with paprika and served alongside white rice flecked with wild rice. It's so nostalgic, but still a bloody great meal. I've added chard to round it out a bit, but spinach works just as well. Feel free to add some wild rice to keep true to the nineties.

SERVES 4

- 4 tablespoons neutral oil (such as groundnut or sunflower)
- 750g (1lb 10oz) mixed mushrooms (button, chestnut and portobello), whole, halved, quartered or sliced, depending on size
- 2 onions, finely sliced
- 5 garlic cloves, finely sliced
- 1 teaspoon paprika (preferably sweet)
- ¼ teaspoon cayenne or chilli powder
- 200ml (7fl oz) white wine or cider
- 300g (10½oz) rainbow chard, leaves separated from stalks, stalks finely sliced, leaves roughly chopped
- 200ml (7fl oz) stock
- 200ml (7fl oz) crème fraîche
- 3 tablespoons lemon juice, or more to taste
- 15g (½oz) parsley or chervil (or both), finely chopped
- sea salt flakes and black pepper
- boiled rice, to serve

1. Heat half the oil in a deep pan large enough to accommodate everything. Fry the mushrooms over a medium heat for 5–7 minutes, turning once or twice, until a good golden brown colour. If they begin to stick, add a splash of water to keep everything moving. Once the mushrooms are coloured well, scoop out and reserve.

2. Add the remaining oil followed by the onions and a good pinch of salt and cook for 12–15 minutes until translucent and soft. Follow with the garlic and give them a stir. Add the mushrooms back in, along with the paprika and cayenne or chilli powder. Stir to combine well in the pan.

3. Add the wine or cider and allow the alcohol to bubble off for 30 seconds. Add the chard stalks along with the stock and cook for 5 minutes. Then add the crème fraîche and allow to bubble away for 2 minutes until slightly thickened.

4. Add the chard leaves and simmer for 3 minutes. Remove from the heat and add the lemon juice with the chopped herbs. Check the seasoning and add more salt if needed. A good grind of black pepper is welcome. Serve spooned on top of rice.

Mushroom tart

The tart can be eaten on its own with a salad, or add pan-fried mushrooms, herbs and crème fraîche to make it a more special dinner offering. I use a long, rectangular flan tin (35 × 11cm/14¼ x 4 inches), but you can also use a 20cm (8 inch), high-sided tart tin or cake tin. The mixed mushrooms definitely benefit from a minimum 40 per cent portobello mushrooms; the darker, inkier gills add a deeper flavour and colour to the end mixture.

SERVES 8

FOR THE PASTRY
- 180g (6oz) wholemeal flour, chilled in the refrigerator, plus extra for dusting
- 90g (3¼oz) unsalted butter, diced and well chilled
- ¼ teaspoon sea salt flakes
- 1 tablespoon cider or white wine vinegar

FOR THE FILLING
- 3 tablespoons neutral oil (such as groundnut or sunflower)
- 1 onion, finely sliced
- 2 garlic cloves, finely sliced
- sprig of thyme, leaves picked
- 1 fresh bay leaf
- 500g (1lb 2oz) chestnut, button and portobello mushrooms, thickly sliced
- 75ml (2½fl oz) white wine or sherry
- 100g (3½oz) crème fraîche
- nutmeg, to taste
- 3 eggs, beaten
- sea salt flakes and black pepper

FOR THE TOPPING (OPTIONAL)
- 2 tablespoons extra-virgin olive oil
- 250g (9oz) wild mushrooms
- 10g (¼oz) parsley, leaves picked and finely chopped
- 10g (¼oz) chives, finely chopped
- 100g (3½oz) crème fraîche to serve

1. To make the pastry, put the flour, butter and salt in a food processor. Pulse until the mix resembles fine breadcrumbs. Add the vinegar and 2 tablespoons of cold water, then pulse a couple more times to combine. Turn out onto a clean work surface and bring the mix together into a mass. Cover and let it sit for 15 minutes.

2. Dust the work surface with flour, place the dough in the middle and sprinkle with some more flour. Roll out the pastry in long strokes going one direction at a time; avoid rolling back and forth over the pastry. The diameter of the dough should be roughly 30cm (12 inches) if using a round tin.

3. Roll the pastry onto the rolling pin. Place a flan tin underneath and roll the pastry over the tin. Lift the edges to let the pastry fall into the tin, then gently coax it into the sides, trying not to stretch the dough. Tuck over any extra pastry that comes over the edge. Place in the refrigerator to rest for 30–45 minutes.

4. Meanwhile in a large, deep pan, heat the oil over a medium heat and add the onions. Cook for 10–15 minutes until soft and translucent.

5. Add the garlic, thyme leaves and bay. Stir to combine, then cook for 2 minutes. Increase the heat to medium-high and add the mushrooms. Stir to incorporate the mushrooms well, then cook for 3–4 minutes, stirring at long intervals to allow the mushrooms to colour, until the mushrooms start to stick. Then add the wine or sherry and bubble for 30 seconds to cook off the alcohol.

6. Once the mushrooms are cooked, remove from the heat. Take out the bay leaf and put the mixture into a blender. Add the crème fraîche, then blend until smooth. Grate in the nutmeg to taste, season with pepper and salt if necessary. Allow to cool to room temperature before assembling the tart.

Or at this stage, put into jars. The residual heat will vacuum seal them and you have a mushroom pâté. I double batch the filling and make both tart and pâté.

7. Preheat the oven to 200°C (400°F), Gas Mark 6. Place the baking beans in the tart case lined with greaseproof paper and bake for 15 minutes. Remove the beans and cook for a further 10 minutes until the case is golden. Remove from the oven and set aside.

8. When ready to assemble, stir the eggs into the mushroom mixture and spoon into the prepared tart case. Spread out to smooth the top. Bake in the oven for 20–30 minutes until set. Give a little shake towards the end of cooking to check where you are at: a little wobble in the centre is good, as the tart will continue to cook once out of the oven.

9. Meanwhile, if you are making the topping, in a frying pan over a high heat, add the oil and fry the mushrooms for about 5 minutes until golden. Add the parsley and chives, stir for 20 seconds and remove from the heat. Season with salt and pepper.

10. Serve the tart cut into slices topped with the wild mushrooms, if using, and a spoon of crème fraîche, if you like.

Stuffed *mushrooms* with breadcrumbs & blue cheese

Hydrating the breadcrumb mix ensures that everything stays moist and is really juicy to eat while still getting a crunchy top. I often prepare the mushrooms ahead of time, set out on a tray ready to go, then bake them when needed. The topping is essentially a blue cheese-spiked stuffing. Comforting and reassuring.

SERVES 4 AS A MAIN WITH SIDES

- 4 tablespoons olive oil
- 2 onions, diced
- 200ml (7fl oz) cider or white wine
- 15g (½oz) parsley, leaves and stalks finely chopped
- 300g (10½oz) fresh breadcrumbs, not too fine, the coarser the better
- 250g (9oz) blue cheese, coarsely grated or roughly chopped
- 8 portobello mushrooms, trimmed
- sea salt flakes and black pepper

1. Preheat the oven to 180°C (350°F), Gas Mark 4.

2. Heat 2 tablespoons of the oil in a pan over a medium heat and add the onion. Cook for 10 minutes until starting to soften. Then add the cider or wine and boil for 30 seconds to evaporate the alcohol. Continue cooking for a further 5 minutes.

3. Remove from the heat and stir in the parsley, followed by the breadcrumbs and cheese. Add 300ml (10fl oz) of water and a decent pinch of salt. Check the seasoning, add pepper and adjust accordingly. The mix should be wet but holding together.

4. Dress the mushrooms in the rest of the oil and a sprinkle of salt. Lay them flat on a baking tray, gills facing up. Fill evenly with the breadcrumb and cheese mixture. Bake in the oven for 25–35 minutes until the mushrooms are cooked through and the tops golden.

index